Soul Food 2:

101 More
Inspirational Messages

liberty forrest

Discover other titles by liberty forrest at

www.libertyforrest.com

ISBN: 1481940228
ISBN-13: 978-1481940221

What people are saying about

liberty forrest's "Soul Food" series:

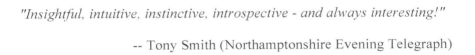

"Insightful, intuitive, instinctive, introspective - and always interesting!"

-- Tony Smith (Northamptonshire Evening Telegraph)

"To say that liberty's writing is 'interesting' is quite an understatement."

-- Sreedharan Shah, Kerala, India

"Reading liberty's inspirational writing is like having my own personal rainbow delivered to me every time."

-- Debra Carney, Florida, USA

.

Table of Contents

INTRODUCTION

What you are about to read originated as posts on my daily inspirational blog. For purposes of this book, I have altered or expanded upon some of the entries. As they have been rearranged, they are out of sequence and therefore, so are the occasional references to holidays, seasons and so on.

Almost all of the entries were written whilst I was living in England, although some are from after I moved back to Calgary, in Western Canada.

Please note: As I have dual nationality, spellings are mainly British, but there may be inconsistencies, as I am also Canadian.

101 INSPIRATIONAL MESSAGES

liberty forrest

1. You only fail when you stop trying to succeed

Is there something you want to do? Some particular goal you have? Perhaps it's a habit you want to break, for example, stopping smoking. Or maybe something you want to learn to do, for example learn to play the piano.

Have you tried to achieve that goal, but stumbled? Stopped smoking only to start again? And again and again and again? Then stopped stopping, gave up trying, resigned to the fact that you're a failure?

Have you tried some sort of new business venture that didn't go according to plan (i.e. didn't work out at all) despite your having been absolutely certain it would be a great success?

Perhaps you haven't even bothered to start trying. One of my favourites is when adults say things like, "I always wanted to play the piano" and I tell them, "So learn." They say they're too old. And I say, "You still have a pulse." And they insist they just couldn't.

Well, I guess if they decide they can't, then they can't. It's really more about "then they won't", because they've made a choice and decided not to even bother trying.

My mother used to shoot me down before I'd even begun to try new things. Right up until she got dementia, she was still telling me, "You can't do that!" when I'd mention something new I wanted to do or learn.

When my children were little, it drove my mother nuts that I used to have confidence in them. My eldest daughter sings beautifully, and when she was 9, she was going to sing at a wedding. I wanted her to stand front and center in the church so she could be seen and heard properly.

My daughter was quite happy with this, knew the lyrics inside out, backwards, upside down and was a very outgoing child, not at all nervous being in such a position.

My mother insisted that she should be way over to one side, behind the piano with the lyrics there for her, just in case. There was a lot of heated discussion about this, in front of my daughter. Unfortunately, that was back before I knew how to stand up for myself and I ended up caving.

As it turned out, people on one side of the church couldn't hear or see Amy very well - and she never did look down at the lyrics...

Amy was disappointed that she hadn't got the opportunity to prove that she could do it - not just to my mother, but to herself. She hadn't been allowed the chance to succeed.

My mother was teaching insecurity and self-doubt, which really bothered me, but it was years before I understood that she was teaching what she knew. In her own way, she was trying to protect my daughter from failing and ending up lacking confidence, which was a major problem in my mother.

As the years passed, I could see that throughout her life, she'd felt like a failure in many ways. She projected a lot of her pain and disappointment onto the people she loved, fearing that they would end up in the same state. She wanted to do and learn and try things but because she lacked confidence, she gave up, often without even having tried.

The bottom line is, you only fail when you stop trying to succeed. So you've stopped smoking 286 times, only to begin again. Is that a good reason to say you've failed? Absolutely not. It just means you haven't been successful at reaching your goal of becoming a non-smoker. Yet.

Whatever your goal is, as long as you keep trying to reach it, there is the chance you will succeed. If you want to be successful, stop thinking of yourself as a failure. You will only fail when you give up and refuse to try again.

2. I love waiting

Yesterday, I had the good fortune to be sitting in a hospital and waiting. While I sat there, it struck me as odd that I used to say "I'm waiting" as though I had a mouth full of barbed wire. It was a nuisance. It was irritating. A complete and utter waste of precious time.

But down the years, I've learned a thing or perhaps even two, and now I rather enjoy waiting.

To be honest, I do not enjoy waiting when it is for something unpleasant, something awful. When you know bad news has packed its suitcase and is on its way to see you or at least has said it might stop by and say hello on its way to visit somewhere else.

But that doesn't mean I enjoy waiting only when it's for something good either, because I've discovered that waiting has a joy all its own. How did I get there?

Well, step one was in learning to tolerate waiting, and that was about being patient.

When you have kids, you spend an awful lot of time waiting. I used to be ridiculously impatient but then I had five children. When you become a parent, you get three choices: become patient, hurl yourself off a bridge, or end up in a room with quilted wallpaper.

Okay, so I learned to tolerate waiting. Did I like it? No. So it still felt like a waste of time. But then I learned the Buddhist art of being mindful. Such a simple concept, but my goodness, how it changes life for the better. When practicing mindfulness, time slows, your body slows, your breath slows, your blood pressure settles. You learn to notice and let go, notice and let go. It's all about observing, watching, drifting peacefully from one moment to the next, as you notice and appreciate each one before moving on to the next

For a very long time, a typical day for me has meant about 18 hours of work. Quite often, it's even 19 and occasionally 20. This includes weekends. It's a good job that for me, "work" is enjoyable and involves being creative, doing things I love.

Because I enjoy what I'm doing for "work", it's easy for me to forget to "play", to goof off, to just chill and do nothing. And so, the Universe gently reminds me to take a break sometimes by offering the blessing of waiting.

Somewhere along the way, I realised that I could use waiting as a mindfulness meditation. It offers an opportunity to notice the lines in the wood grain on the floor and see how pretty they are. And let the thought go. It's an opportunity to notice the birds' cheerful song...and let it go. The sound of passing cars...and let it go. The way the chair feels under you...and let it go.

You notice the snippets of conversation between people who are sitting nearby, and let them go. You notice your body, the feel of your tongue as it rests in your mouth, your elbows as they touch the chair, the slow and gentle rise and fall of your tummy as you take each breath. And you let each thought go as it gives way to the next and the next, noticing and letting go.

The more you notice and let go, the more you relax. Anxiety is worry about the future, so as you stay in the 'here and now', anxious thoughts melt away because you know that all your remaining moments will take care of themselves as you get to them. For right here, right now, in this very moment, all is well.

And if all isn't well, you let go of those thoughts as you focus on all your other experiences in this moment, and you know that your life in this moment is not just about the pain. Like every other moment, the painful ones will all pass too.

The more you focus on what you experience right here and right now, the more present you are in your life. If you're thinking about ten minutes from now, or tomorrow, or next week, or when you retired, you're missing what's happening in your life right now, in this moment.

If you're thinking about earlier this morning, or late last night, or last week, or 27 years ago, you're missing what's happening in your life right now, in this moment.

Being mindful allows you to stay connected with yourself and your life. All it takes is a constant flow of noticing and letting go of what was noticed.

An excellent place to begin practicing mindfulness is when you're eating. Notice every detail, as you raise your arm and use your hand to pick up the fork. Marvel at your body and how amazing it is that you're able to do this - especially when some cannot.

Notice the fork as you hold it between your fingers. Notice how your mouth begins to water as you scoop food onto the fork. Notice the aroma of the food. Look at it. Think about where it came from, how many processes and people it took to get it from where it began until it landed on your plate, from people who planted seeds to people driving the lorries to get the food to the shops - and the workers there, too.

As you raise the fork toward you, notice your mouth opening. Notice where your tongue is as the food goes into your mouth. Pay attention to your lips closing around the fork, and how they feel as it slides back out of your mouth. Notice the texture of the food and everything that happens in your mouth as you chew.

I could go on but I'm sure you get the point. The more detailed you are in being mindful, the more benefit you will derive, as it improves overall health and well-being. It brings clarity of focus and thinking, improves concentration, deepens insight and intuitive wisdom, increases resilience to change, strengthens relationships and improves self-confidence.

It can significantly reduce stress which offers many health benefits all by itself.

I'm so grateful that now I see "waiting" as a delicious opportunity to be mindful. I accept it as the Universe gently offering a respite from my long work days. No longer does it feel like barbed wire in my mouth. No longer do I see "waiting" as doing nothing, or a monumental waste of precious time.

Oh, no. Not at all. Now, I'm happy to say, as though it is a most important job, "I'm waiting." And it is a most important job because it affords me the opportunity to be mindful of every moment of my life.

3. No "me time"? Try this - and no more excuses

Recently, a few friends have been telling me about how insanely busy they are. They say, "I have no 'me time' at all!"

They're exhausted. Fed up with responsibilities, everyone and everything else coming first, needing attention.

Well, the truth is, if everyone and everything else is coming first, it's only because these friends are allowing it. You don't just "find time" for yourself. You have to create it.

Of course there are certain obligations that must be met which mean you have to be here or do that at certain times. But there's a difference between those (eg. being sure children get to school on time, or you show up to your job etc) and how you fill your other hours (eg evenings and weekends).

I spent a lot of years being a single parent. Part of the time it was with five children, while I was juggling five part-time jobs - and serious illness and some other personal issues that placed huge demands on my time and energy. I understand "busy".

In spite of all that, I always made time for myself. As I told my very busy friends recently, it doesn't have to take a lot of minutes to yourself every day to make a big difference in your life. They lobbed their doubtful responses in my direction but I was not deterred.

I told them about one of my favourite mini-meditations. It involves a very short period of time, preferably first thing when you get up each day. You can get up a few minutes earlier - 15 would be nice. Ten is good. Five is better than a kick in the backside with a frozen mukluk. Or a soggy moccasin.

Now don't tell me you can't manage 5-10 minutes each day for yourself. I'm just not buying it. You can. If you won't, that's another story.

So - get up a few minutes earlier. Yes, even if you're already getting up at 5 or 5.30. I've been sleep-deprived for 36 years and I'm still breathing. Some things are just worth it.

I used to get up at that hour every day, even on weekends before my children got up, just so I could spend nearly two hours on yoga, meditating etc. every day because after doing it for a short time, I could see what a massive difference it made to my life. The benefits far outweighed losing a bit of sleep.

Anyway, I'm not suggesting you spend two hours every morning doing yoga and meditation (although you certainly could if you felt so inclined!).

No, I'm going to tell you what I suggested to my very busy friends. It's a simple and lovely little thing called a candle meditation. As soon as you climb out of bed and are still in that lovely half-awake state, find your way to a darkened room if possible.

Light a candle. Sit quietly and look at the flame. Just focus on how beautiful it is, how gentle, how peaceful its movements are, softly flickering, dancing... It moves with the air. Focus on your breathing in a way that is designed to cause as little air movement and flame-flickering as possible. Think "stillness" as you try to keep the flame from moving by taking slow, deep, even breaths.

Or just look at the flame. But don't sit there stewing about your problems and worries. Just look at the flame. Focus on it, watch what it does, see how it moves. Notice colours in it, watch the edges of the candle change shape as the wax slowly melts.

If you're going to think about anything while gazing at your candle, think of gratitude. Think of the blessings in your life. Think of positive things, and only positive things.

Do this candle meditation every morning for a couple of weeks. Or do it before you go to bed but do it consistently; give it a real chance. Don't tell me you haven't got time.

If you think you're unable to give yourself 5 or 10 minutes a day, you're making far too many excuses to sabotage your own life and happiness. If you're so important that you have to get all that other 'stuff' done, then you're important enough to take care of yourself.

So get up (or get ready for bed) a little early. Sit quietly and watch the flame of a candle for a few minutes. You'll enjoy it. You'll begin to look forward to it. You'll want more of this, or some other bit of 'me time' to journal, to read, to do 5-10 mins of yoga - whatever. You'll miss it if you skip a day. So don't.

No more excuses.

4. Be nice. And forget about the outcome.

I was chatting with a friend recently. She was really upset because despite her best efforts to be kind and respectful in a particular situation, she was treated pretty badly in return. I could sense her bewilderment, her confusion as she wondered why this had happened. There was a childlike innocence in the way she'd been expecting that being nice would have got her the same in return. Or at least, in her distress about the fact that being nice did not get her the same in return.

It was rather like seeing a child open a lovely birthday present and find a toy she'd wanted forever, and then discovering that it was broken. She said something like, "I was minding The Golden Rule, being as nice as I could be and I don't understand why they treated me like this anyway!"

Well, I guess I could say a few things in response to that. The first is that understanding it doesn't change the fact that it happened. Even if someone has had a terrible day, just received awful news, for example, and rips your head off for no apparent reason, that person is still responsible for his or her actions. There is no way to take back hurtful words or actions.

The next thing I would say is that you don't have any control over what other people do or don't do. Honey may attract more flies than vinegar but ultimately, the fly still gets to do the choosing. Just because you're being sweet, it doesn't mean you'll get what you want or that you'll be treated with the same respect as you are giving.

But to be honest, I think the biggest problem with my friend's situation, and the millions of others who have the same experience, is that they're misunderstanding or misinterpreting The Golden Rule.

Look at what it says: "Do unto others as you would have them do unto you."

It's suggesting that we treat people a particular way. Full stop.

But somewhere along the way, a whole other section has been added: "And then people will do unto you as you did unto them."

In reality, it says nothing at all about the other person's actions. The focus is only on what we should do. Yet for some reason, we seem to think that those words contain the promise of a pleasant reaction in all cases every time we're nice to other people. And so we're surprised or bewildered when it doesn't go that way. We feel hurt and disappointed, and sometimes wonder what we did wrong, or what we did to warrant such treatment.

But nowhere in The Golden Rule is there anything that should lead us to the expectation that other people should behave in a particular way because of something we do or don't do. If you think about it, that's rather arrogant (and somewhat controlling) of us to decide what is the correct way for someone else to behave in a given situation. It says "You do not have the right to free will – but I do." It says, "I made my own choice but I am not letting you make yours."

It is unreasonable to project your reactions, responses and sensibilities onto others. It is a mistake to expect people to give you the same consideration, courtesy and respect that you naturally give them because quite often, they won't. Don't slide into the comfortable illusion that everyone else will be as nice to you as you have been to them. Accept that no matter how respectful you are to other people in the first place, they are free to be as rotten to you as they want. Be prepared for it, so if and when it happens, you aren't disappointed, hurt or bewildered.

I'm not suggesting that you should *expect* them to be rotten. It's just that having expectations of any kind is unreasonable and unfair. It also means you're inviting disappointment, at the very least.

It's great to do your best to be kind and respectful to other people, but be sure that you don't take it personally or feel crushed when you don't get the same in return. To me, that's just sensible, and it saves an awful lot of grief.

5. Sometimes you have to break the vase

I've had a good, solid kick in the guts recently. The kind that knocks the stuffing out of you. The kind that sends you reeling and leaves your head spinning.

It was the kind of kick that is so hard, it shakes loose your entire belief system, right down to your core, rattling every last bit of hope and certainty you ever had until they're smashed to pieces.

I got up after the first kick, brushed the twigs and dirt off my clothes and carried on. Then I got a really brutal kick. It was much worst than the first. I wasn't gonna get up again. Figured there was no point.

But I dried my eyes, took a deep breath, and stood up. I decided that it had just been a test of faith, and as I'm perfectionistic about tests, I wasn't gonna do an "A-". It had to be an "A" and therefore, I would prove that my faith was strong and solid.

So I squared my shoulders, laughed off the two solid kicks, and smiled, thinking "Bring it on!"

Okay, I guess them was fightin' words. I reckon I asked for the next kick. And the one after that. And I suspect there will be several more in the near future. I had the Universe pegged as more of a chess-player than a kick-boxer but apparently, I was wrong. Just one of many lessons in this whole situation.

When I was first looking at this test of faith, it was like I was looking at my spiritual beliefs as a strong and solid marble vase. I've relied on a particular set of beliefs for a long time, and although there were some additions and deletions of various specific parts down the years, the fundamental structure has not wavered. That marble vase held all the fresh water and beautiful flowers I could put in it. I needed that vase because for me, life just isn't worth living without being able to enjoy the magnificent beauty of the flowers that it contained.

I loved my marble vase. It was perfect. I made it myself. I'd worked so hard on it and it had taken a few decades to create it, so it suited me exactly. It was so strong and solid, it never occurred to me that anything could break it. Or that anything would be horrible enough to try.

Although marble is extremely solid and durable, it is possible to crack it if you drop something extremely heavy on it. Well, that's what's happened to my beautiful vase in the past couple of weeks, and the marble cracked. I continued pouring in lots of water to try to keep the flowers alive, but the water kept leaking out faster than I could refill the vase. The closer I looked, the more cracks I saw. And the flowers began to die.

At various points in this experience, I tried using epoxy adhesive to repair the cracks, but more appeared in other places. I'd got to the point of thinking the entire vase needed to be chucked. Not only did I not want to look at the vase any more, I didn't even want to look at marble.

In fact, it got so bad, I was questioning whether or not I even wanted another vase.

This morning I heard a light rain beginning to fall. I went out to my secluded garden, needing connection with nature, with Mother Earth and the Universe in which she lives.

I sat on the patio, listening to the quiet wisdom of the herbs, the flowers, the thick ivy that covers the lattice fence. I felt the raindrops on my skin, appreciating that every one of them came from the heavens, a subtle yet powerful message about my connection with the Divine – that we are all spiritual beings and we are all connected to one another.

In such perfect surroundings, the answers began to come.

I remembered life before the vase. I remembered the horrible, dark feeling of being completely and utterly lost and alone, without spiritual beliefs, without that connection to the Divine, and to everyone else.

I knew I must look at the cracked marble vase again. I thought maybe I needed to wait until the last kick in the guts had been delivered. I wondered if perhaps I must let the cracks stop forming before deciding what to do.

The way I saw it, I had only two choices. I could haul out the epoxy, repair the cracks and when I'd look at my beautiful vase, I would see them as 'war wounds', symbols of surviving my test of faith.

Or I could take a hammer to my marble vase and break it into pieces. I could put them together in a different way, perhaps using only some of them and connecting those pieces with beautiful bits of coloured glass or pretty stones. I could still see something of my original vase, but it would just be different. It might even be more beautiful than the original. And it would, in all likelihood, be much stronger than the first.

I thought that perhaps I must endure the rest of the kicks before I will be able to make a decision about whether I need the adhesive or the hammer. I suspect – no, I am quite certain – that it is the latter. A daunting consideration, to say the least, but that must be irrelevant.

And it has occurred to me that perhaps – and quite probably – making the decision now might just prevent further kicks.

But one thing I know for sure, whatever it will look like, I do need a vase. It is the whole point, the purpose, the reason for my existence.

So I will haul out the hammer, find the coloured bits of glass and the pretty stones. I will choose the best pieces of my lovely old marble vase and I will create another that is unique and even stronger than the last. It is daunting, yes, and even rather frightening to contemplate tearing apart my entire belief system, starting from scratch and constructing a new one.

It's not the first time I've done it. I survived it once. I'm sure I'll survive it again.

6. Who or what is important to you?

I'd like you to grab a piece of paper and write down your answers to a few questions I'm about to ask. It'll be important in a minute, you'll see. So I'll wait........

Okay. Ready?

What is important to you? Don't read any further, please, until you've written your answer. It doesn't have to be lengthy or involved, just a quick point form list will do.

This little exercise can be quite a profound experience if you do it, so please do yourself a favour and take a few moments with this

Okay. Next question. Who is important to you? Another quick point form list, please.

Now, a separate list. Please jot down what has eaten up your week. Make a few notes about how you spent your time over the past seven days. What were you doing each day?

One more thing: What were you thinking about during the week? What was on your mind?

I really hope you wrote those answers down because there's something about seeing them in writing that works better than just leaving it all in your head.

Now, please take a look at your list of what you did and what you thought about for the past week. Most people have a whole lot of stuff on their lists that is about work – whether it's about their jobs or the housework, the errands, the obligations, the responsibilities, the meetings, the children's homework and music lessons and the groceries and the meals blah blah blah.

Okay, let's take a look at your list of what is important to you. Chances are, some of that stuff is on that list, as it should be. But are there things on that list that aren't getting your attention? Why not?

Look at the list of who is important to you. Did those people make it onto your list of how you spent your time and what you were thinking about?

If there is something incongruent about all of this, perhaps you could stand a shift in your priorities. If you say it's important to play and enjoy your life more, then do it. If you say your children, your parents, your sister, your friends are important to you, then make sure they know it. Write. Phone. Email. Send a card. Organise spending time together.

And don't forget: You should really be on that list of who is important to you. If you're not, then put yourself right at the top and make sure you spend time doing something for yourself every day, even if it's only for 10 or 15 minutes.

We give our attention to what is important to us. Sometimes we know what should be important, and we can say all the right stuff on that subject, but really, in our heart of hearts, our priorities are a mess.

It's another case of actions speaking louder than words. If you say something or someone is important to you, then show it. Prove it. Live it. No more excuses.

7. You can learn a lot from children

I love children. They're just too cool. They know what we "Grown Up" People have forgotten. They know what's important and we can learn a lot from them – if we so choose.

There's nothing quite like watching the wheels turning in an intelligent young mind that is curious and soaking up a load of new information. I love seeing those bright eyes so focused – just like lasers as they watch and learn.

I love the way children bubble over with enthusiasm. Some are like a pot of homemade soup that's a little too full, boiling and rolling with big, bloopy, bubbles of chunky vegetables and fresh herbs that spill over and sizzle on the hob. Others are bright, quick and sparkling, fizzing over the top like the finest champagne

Quite naturally, children love to play and we spend a good deal of time teaching them not to do it. Sit down. Be quiet. Do your chores. Do your homework. Make your bed. Mow the lawn. Don't be silly. Mind your manners. Settle down. Shhhhhhh!

We teach them to work hard. To be ambitious. To get ahead. To "make something of themselves", as if they are nothing in the first place. In fact, they are pure and perfect to begin with, but along with Life, we knock it out of them and turn them into joyless, responsible adults who've forgotten how to dream, how to share, how to remember that it's not whether you win or lose, but how you play the game.

I've been watching "Junior Masterchef Australia" the past couple of weeks and have been astonished by children, aged 8-12, cooking things I can't pronounce, using ingredients I've never heard of, plating up dishes that look like they were served in a 5-star restaurant. As if that hasn't been enough of a treat, it's been extra wonderful to see some very important differences between them and the adults who I've seen on two seasons of the adult version of the same show.

In the team challenges on the grown-up version, one person will have won a challenge, and that person will be a team captain. Let's say it's a man who has won. He is allowed to choose the other team captain, and he does it strategically, choosing someone he thinks will be a poor captain, causing the other team to lose the challenge, because one member of that team will be eliminated from the competition.

Then for his team members, he selects the people he believes are the best contestants because he wants to stay in the competition, win the title, win the $100,000 and the cookbook deal.

But on Junior Masterchef, it's another story. When a little boy won a challenge and was going to be team captain, he got to choose the other captain. When asked why he chose a particular boy, there was nothing strategic about it, and certainly nothing to do with ensuring that his own team would win. "He's my mate and I thought he'd like it," he said.

When the adults are doing team challenges, members from one team look nervously over at everyone on the other one, to see who's in the lead. They're panicking, stressed, freaking out, worried, constantly blathering on about how they *cannot* lose this challenge because they *really wanna win!* They're sweating and frantic, the adrenalin's gotta be a killer. And they sure as heck don't look like they're having any fun at all.

One of the kids' team challenges was for each team to put up three dishes for a school cafeteria at lunchtime. During the challenge, kids from one team were encouraging – and even helping – the other team when it was lagging a little, and in danger of not finishing the dishes for the students.

It felt like one big, enjoyable team effort that was all about making sure everyone finished on time so the students would not be disappointed. It didn't feel at all like two separate teams that were meant to be about working for points, which would ultimately affect each contestant's standing in the competition. And the kids were having an awful lot of fun.

When the judges praised the adults' dishes, quite often the other contestants looked jealous or worried. They'd plaster fake smiles on their faces, gritting their teeth while clapping with all the enthusiasm of a bunch of writhing fish hanging by hooks in their faces.

When the judges praise the children's dishes, the other kids light up.

They're beaming. They're so excited, hugging each other and saying, "You did a great job!" and obviously meaning every little bit of their excitement and pure affection.

When the adults got eliminated, most of them were very upset. Some were even quite obviously angry, especially as they got down to the wire and were very close to having won. They tried to choke it down, but it was clearly written on their pained faces. And when they were back just days later to watch the two finalists compete, you could still see the disappointment, the anger, the jealousy. There were only fake smiles and false encouragement for the finalists.

When the children are eliminated, they say, "Out of 5,500 kids who applied, I can't believe I got this far! I'm really proud/happy/excited about that!" They're still beaming, radiant, thrilled when they get their trophies and they don't care that they just lost out on several thousand dollars in a trust fund and the title of the first ever Junior Masterchef Australia. They're just genuinely happy for getting as far as they did. And they're genuinely happy for the contestants who are still 'in'.

The adults are all about the fame, the title, the money, the winning, going on about this being 'their only chance' to open their own restaurant etc.

Well, how did all the other restaurants in the world happen?? Did everyone have to win a competition that would give them some start-up money? Ummm, I don't think so. Too much hype and too much rubbish about winning has made them lose their perspective completely.

The kids are happy to see the others succeed and it's not about whether you win or lose, it's how you play the game. They know it's supposed to be about fun, about having a really cool experience, about learning, about supporting each other. It's about enjoying the ride and not worrying about the destination.

Yup. You can learn a lot from children.

8. What you do tells the world who you are

Yes, it's true. Actions do speak louder than words. In fact, they scream into a megaphone.

You might hear people tell you how "spiritual" or "religious" they are. Then they throw judgement around like a volleyball. They gossip more than Mrs Olsen did on "Little House on the Prairie". They insult, criticise and look down their self-righteous noses every chance they get.

You might hear people tell you how much they respect themselves. Then you hear them make self-deprecating comments. You watch them eat nothing but fat and sugar. They drink excessively.

Or they're sliding into bed with one person after another after another at the drop of a hat – or a pair of trousers. And perhaps, not being very 'safe' about it either.

You might hear people tell you they're your friends and you believe they really care about you. But when you're ill or struggling through a bad time, they're nowhere to be seen and can't even be bothered to ring to see how you're doing.

Or perhaps you hear of people who tell you of their Really Big Dreams. They go on at length about how they're going to do this and that, and they make loads of detailed plans.

But then, apart from talking about them, they never actually do anything toward putting them into action.

You might have a boyfriend who tells you how devastated he was by a girlfriend who cheated on him in the past. He swears up and down that he would never – could never – do that to anyone and then you find out he's cheating on you, and he's done it to virtually everyone before you.

You hear people say they hate liars. Yet you have personal experience of the countless times they've been dishonest.

You hear people tell you how strong and brave they are, how confident, and then they don't dare go for that promotion because they're sure they won't get it. They won't stand up to the shop owner who was rude. They let fear make their choices for them and their insecurity oozes out of every bit of hesitation and questioning.

Whatever you say, it's what you do that will tell the world the truth about who you are. You may fool people for a while, especially if they're particularly trusting, or prone to giving people the benefit of the doubt. But in the end, there's really nowhere to hide.

Even if you never said another word, your intentions and your true feelings would be screaming like a banshee.

In the end, everything you do will tell people whether or not you mean what you say. And they will react accordingly.

What do your actions say about you? Or more to the point, what do you want them to say?

9. If you woke up and knew that this was your last day...

...what would you do?

Yeah, okay, I'm sure most of us would want to spend every last moment with our loved ones – or at least, have them with us while we hurry up and cram everything we can manage into one last day.

It's all very romantic and lovely to imagine quietly sitting with our loved ones while we peacefully fade away. But what about the Other Stuff? Wouldn't there be a list of Other Stuff that we wish we could do, too?

I don't know about you, but after those first powerful thoughts of wanting to be with my family and closest friends, my next thought would be to get rid of everything I don't want people to find.

First – and most importantly – the underwear. I can just see myself, tearing through my drawers of Victoria's Secret knickers and such, thinking "What a waste!" as I'm chucking all that expensive lace into the bin! And I can hear my mother on the other side, watching this and saying, "See? Now you know why I made you promise to throw out all my underwear immediately upon my death!"

I can see myself digging through stacks of notebooks and paperwork, because as a writer, sometimes I blather on at length to myself about my very most personal stuff and wouldn't want to horrify my loved ones posthumously. Bad enough when I've done it in this life, but at least I get to apologise – or at least explain myself!

I'd make quite a nice little fire with all those papers. More like a bonfire, really. It's much nicer to admire the flames than be annoyed by the buzzing of a paper shredder. If I could stand marshmallows, it'd be a great chance to put some on a stick and roast 'em but they are far too gross for words.

Ew.

I'd have to do a quick clean and tidy of my house, which is usually not in terrible shape anyway because I don't function well in chaotic, messy surroundings. But as they say you should always leave a place tidier than you found it, so if I'm seriously leaving, then I ought to make an effort!

I'd go to the nearest jewellery store and buy as much yummy stuff as I could get on my visa (which would be paid back out of my estate so nothing illegal there!). I've always loved beautiful sparkly stuff but haven't had much of it in my life. And I'd seriously be takin' it with me, too, as I just bought it, so I'd wear it all, whether it matches or not.

After my shopping spree, I'd stop for something really awful like a Burger King Whopper with bacon and cheese, onion rings too please. Then I'd do a takeaway pizza (to eat later after all that Burger Kingness).

I'd soak in a hot bubble bath, scrubbing as much of the dead stuff off my heels as possible so as not to accidentally carve up the undertaker, if he should have occasion to touch my feet. I'd be washing my hair, to save him the trouble, and of course would be doing my nails (toenails, too, as always). For many years, it's been one of my simplest and most favourite pleasures.

I'd get into my most comfortable "jams" (is there any other attire that's appropriate for lounging around in the Afterlife?). My new jewellery would definitely not match my jams, but I wouldn't give a rat's @$$ now, would I? It would be delicious in the moment - and really, the moment we are in is the only one that we ever really have.

I'd definitely be playing my favourite music throughout the background of all this soaking, tidying, heel-scraping, burger-eating, last-dayness, with Enigma being at the top of the list. And I'd just have to tickle the ivories for a while, one last time. A bit of Chopin would be in order (he's my fave) and of course the Moonlight Sonata by the painfully serious Beethoven.

And I'd just have to crawl into my deliciously soft bed and watch 'Chicken Run' one last time, too, preferably with my kids and grandchildren, too (with five of each, I'd better get a bigger bed). A good time to eat the pizza!

Oooo, colouring! I'd have to haul out the crayons and colouring books, which we could enjoy with our pizza and Chicken Run.

Does wine go with colouring books? (Yessssssssssss!!!!! if you're old enough, of course. My driving licence says I am but the rest of me thinks

I'm four.)

I'd be so excited, knowing I wouldn't have to bother with flossing any more, or worrying about the fact that I should be doing it when I'm not. That'd be worth doing a little happy dance. Yuck. I hate flossing. But I do it religiously every night.

You know, aside from the obvious need to see or be on the phone with loved ones at such a time, I'm struggling to think of anything else I'd really want to cram into my last day.

Perhaps write a few final thoughts or do one last painting that was colourful and vibrant, summing up the joy I feel about my life (miserable bits included, because they've added to the joy in their own bizarre way).

But really, it would be a day just like any other. I value every one of my days as if it's my last because the truth is, I never know which one that will be. Apart from chucking my knickers and burning my journals (those'll be your jobs, Willow!), I'm pretty much ready to go. I mean, I'm at peace about the whole idea, but I hope it's not for a very long time 'cause I'm quite happy to be here as I'm having way too much fun.

I just don't feel like there's anything big and spectacular that I need to do before I leave this life. I want as much time as possible with people I love. I want to be creative and make people laugh and give them hugs. I want to enjoy the simple things that bring me so much pleasure – the pretty nails, the yummy pizza, or Chicken Run.

I wanna be torched so as not to take up perfectly good space on the planet when I wouldn't really be using it. I heard a few years ago that now you can have your ashes made into diamonds (people can even choose the colour they want) and that's what I'd like to have done to mine.

As I said on my blog some time ago, pick the word that describes how you want to be remembered and live it. Be it. Do it. I said my word was 'sparkle'. It's very cool that I'll be able to sparkle long after I'm gone…

In the meantime, I want to have fun and be silly. I want to make delicious memories with people who will keep them safe for me after I'm gone.

What else is there, really, but the memories we leave behind?

10. Your prayers are always answered. But sometimes, the answer is "No."

I had a plan. It didn't seem to be working. I couldn't understand how something that felt so right when I planned it could turn out to be so wrong.

I took a few guesses at why it wasn't working and tried to fix each one but the more I tried to fix it, the more wrong it seemed to become.

But was it really wrong? Had I missed something I could fix? Or had it initially been perfect just the way it was, with a Higher Purpose being served by my plan appearing to be a complete and utter failure?

With these and many other questions rolling through my mind, and even more possible answers, I grew more confused by the minute as every possible answer threw out a growing list of suggested courses of action.

Changing the plan hadn't worked so it looked like I should abandon it altogether, at least for the time being, and in the specific circumstances.

But that felt like failure to me. Like giving up, admitting defeat, all of which go completely against my grain.

But had I really failed? No. I had to understand that I was selling diamonds in Walmart. There may have been a few diamond-loving customers in the shop but they didn't happen to pass by my little stand while I was there.

That wasn't my fault and it didn't mean no one liked or wanted my diamonds. There was nothing wrong with my diamonds. And there was nothing wrong with the Walmart shoppers. So failure had nothing to do with it.

Well, then, if I packed up my little stand and left before closing, was I giving up?

No. I was accepting that Walmart shoppers aren't looking for diamonds.

Or they might wander past, love the sparkle, think they're beautiful – but diamonds wouldn't go with their everyday clothing, so they're still just window-shopping and trying to imagine themselves actually wearing diamonds someday.

Was I admitting defeat? No. I wasn't doing battle with anyone or anything so it wasn't about that.

So I went back to the beginning. I looked at my plan. In and of itself, it was a great plan. I looked at all its components – my intentions, the whole point, what I was trying to do. Nope, I couldn't see anything wrong in any of that.

And as it seemed that the more I changed it, the worse things got, I decided that it must have been a lot closer to "right" when I started. I couldn't have been so wrong after all.

But I really needed and wanted my plan to work. I'd been so sure it would. So very, absolutely, 100% certain. And an awful lot was riding on my plan.

So when it looked like it was going to fall apart, I prayed for it to be okay. I insisted it would be fine. I was determined to continue, whatever the outcome. I waited for an answer to my prayers.

Finally, the answer came. And it was "No."

Okay. I've parented five children. I've had to say "No", too. I always had good reasons for it, whether or not my children understood what they were.

And as they say, when a door closes, a window opens. So I'm busy looking out that window to see what I can see.

I see that my plan did not fail. I did not give up. I was not defeated. My plan provided me with valuable lessons I needed to learn if I was going to progress, so how could that be wrong or a failure?

It had to be exactly the way it was, even if I still don't know all the reasons why – and I accept that I don't have to know all of them – but that's only because I understand that it's part of a much bigger puzzle.

I have not abandoned or given up on my plan. It is merely in a state of great transformation. And one day, it will become an even more beautiful diamond.

11. So...you want to give up. And then what?

You want to give up. Okay. I can relate to that. But first, be very clear about one thing: there's a big difference between 'giving up' and accepting that a situation will not be improved by your further efforts - and sometimes, to continue might even be to your detriment. The trick is in figuring out which is which.

If you do give up, what will happen? Or what won't happen? And can you live with whatever that is? Will it keep you stuck and not allow you to move forward?

If you're thinking about giving up, I'll bet you're really tired. I can relate to that, too. But is that the reason you want to give up? Being tired can distort your perception of things. It can make everything seem bigger, worse, heavier, more. So if you think that's a big part of why you want to give up, perhaps you could just take a rest instead.

Maybe you're feeling like one of those inflatable bowling-pin shaped things that kids punch in the face so it falls over, but then it springs back up. Maybe you've been punched so often, you're deflated, flattened, and you think you can't get back up yet again.

Yeah, I can relate to that, too.

So haul out the repair kit, patch up the tear, and get up again. I'm well aware that in doing so, you're essentially saying to the Universe, "Okay! Bring it on! Slam me again!"

But even if all you get is flattened one more time, you can still pop back up again. And again. And again. You just have to decide to do it. Yeah, I know you might have reached a point where you really don't want to, and you're asking me, why do you have to decide to do it?

29

It's quite simple really. Life sucks if you just stay there, deflated and miserable on the floor. If you get back up and try again, there is always the chance for improvement. If you don't, there isn't. Yes, you might get knocked down again but so what? It sucks, I know, but is that a good reason to stop trying? To accept that it sucks and sit there and complain about how miserable things are?

I guess that's your choice, but if you want to feel better, then you *have* to try again, until you are quite clearly shown that it's time to stop and do something else instead.

Sooner or later, the Universe will get bored with your refusal to give up. Or you'll learn to brace yourself for the punches and not get knocked down and then you'll be punching the air and yelling, "Checkmate!"

But at the minute, your king's in peril. Your pawns are almost gone. And you've lost a bishop and a rook. Yet you've still got your queen.

Do you really expect life to be easy? Okay, so maybe you're thinking it didn't have to be this hard. Well, I have no answers about why it is. I can speculate, but it doesn't really mean anything in the grand scheme of things. Whatever possible reasons we come up with as to why life has to be so impossibly miserable sometimes are really just our helpless human ramblings, our feeble attempts at making ourselves feel better.

We don't know whether it's all 'meant to be' or random, meaningless misery without a point. We don't know whether we choose this stuff before we get here or whether it's dumped on us by some Supreme Being who has decided it for us. We don't know if it's fate or free will or a little of both. We can guess, we can believe, but we do not really *know*.

And even if we did, would it change anything? Your life would still unfold as it's going to unfold, whatever that means, and however it happens. Hating it because it's hard, or being fed up and tired because it's nothing but struggle - none of that will change even if you get some Big Brilliant Flash of Awareness with a personal memo from the Divine Source of All.

You're still going to have to put one foot in front of the other and get through your life, one day at a time. Or one minute at a time, when it gets really bumpy.

So what are you going to do with those days? Those minutes? Do you really think that giving up on the harder parts of life will make the rest of it any better? Do you really think that if you look at your challenges and say, "I can't! I quit!" that whatever comes after will be better than it is now?

I rather doubt it. Because I'll bet that whatever it is you're trying to do, whatever it is that you want to give up on was designed to make the rest of your life better in some way. It would enhance, improve, or lead to something. Whether it's big or small, you wouldn't have been bothering if there wasn't going to be some benefit for you.

So why would you throw that away, unless you're absolutely certain that you've done all you can do, and that it is really and truly time to accept that you cannot do any more, and stop trying?

The bottom line is this: If accepting the situation and stopping is best for you, if continuing means you're flogging a dead horse which will only prevent you from moving forward (and may, in fact, be detrimental to you) then do it. But if you just can't be bothered to try again, or if you're just tired, slow down. Take a rest

Look at the situation. Forget the pieces you've lost and remember your remaining bishop, your rook, those few pawns. Remember your queen and how much power she wields. Then plot her next move.

And don't stop until it's the right thing to do.

12. Brown thumbs and bootleggin' - how does your garden grow?

Historically, if I could do something the hard way, I did it. If I could find a way to be more misunderstood than I was already, I found it. If I could make my life more difficult, when I was trying to make it easier, I did that, too.

It was just like busting my backside to grow a beautiful garden, and then trampling the pretty little buds while planting bindweed everywhere. That stuff is insane. Just this side of impossible to kill or remove. It's extremely invasive and suffocating and even the tiniest bits of roots can turn into yet another crawling, choking, intrusive plant.

And bramble. Oh, man. The seeds were sown for me when I was very little. It climbs and hides, creeping and crawling everywhere, tearing clothing, tearing flesh with its evil spikes and every time you think you've got rid of it, it reappears in a heartbeat, ignoring you completely, as if it had never been gone.

Sometimes I wasn't battling bindweed and bramble though. Just some happy little misunderstood dandelions that looked so innocuous and pretty, a bright splash of perky yellowness here and there, trying to brighten up the garden, what could be the harm? Well, they can get pretty big and because they spread so quickly and easily, they can brighten it up just a little too much.

Yeah, I know, they have some good uses but I'm talking about having them turn up when and where you don't want them, just like a whole passel of uninvited relatives appearing on your doorstep, steamer trunks in hand and askin' if they can 'set a spell'.

There they are, all tired and sagging, a red-faced Aunt Marjory and toothless

Uncle Herbert, with scrawny cousin Alma and her dim-witted husband, Melvin with their nine dirty, scruffy little offspring who are fighting and shoving each other on your front lawn.

"We ain't got no place ta sleep! We done bin kicked outta the trailer fer not payin' the rent but it ain't mah fault that the bootleggin' moonshine market ain't great and I cain't make no money!" cries Uncle Herbert.

You might not mind them in their trailer, and you might even enjoy a little blast of Uncle Herbert's moonshine now and then (although it'll peel the bark off yer innards). But this is a little too close for comfort.

As a child, I was the seed of a rose bush, buried in a garden full of invasive and suffocating bindweed whose beautiful, deceptive flowers fooled the untrained observer, as did the delicious bramble fruit.

As an adult, I saw them for what they were, and spent decades trying to get rid of them, and all the other weeds that were springing up and doing their level best to destroy the garden I was working so hard to create.

For every lovely plant I managed to nurture until it began to bloom, there were several unwanted and toxic weeds trying to destroy the peaceful, tranquil, beautiful garden for which I yearned.

Still, I kept planting many different flowers and herbs, with countless colours, shapes, sizes and textures, while learning more about the bindweed and bramble, how to dig up their roots and destroy any remaining bit of them that lurked in the soil of my developing garden.

Dandelions and numerous other weeds kept springing up - and they are still springing up here and there. I suppose they always will, because Life is just like that. But my previously very shrivelled brown thumb has gradually become greener over the years as I've become better at guarding and nurturing the plants I want, and removing or preventing the growth of the ones that ruin my garden.

No doubt you can relate to much of what I'm saying. No doubt you have been hoeing and digging, planting and nurturing, doing your best to create a beautiful garden of loveliness in your life, while doing battle with the bindweed, the bramble, the thistles and thorns - and the Aunt Marjorys and Uncle Herberts of your life, the stuff that comes up disguised as relatively harmless but it still ruins your garden.

But if you keep focusing on what you want to create, if you keep a clear vision of that vast array of herbs and flowers, the colours and textures, that lovely, thriving garden that is how you want your life to be, you'll get better at making it happen.

And if you keep studying about how to deal with the bindweed, the bramble, the thistles and thorns, if you keep learning about the conditions in which they thrive - or they don't - then you will get better at keeping them out of your pretty garden.

It doesn't happen overnight. Even the best gardeners weren't born with the knowledge they possess. Some may have more of a knack for it than others, but they still had to learn, although it may have been fairly quick and relatively simple, at least as compared with us brown-thumbers.

And for those of us with the very brownest of thumbs, who just seemed to create one major disaster after another throughout our lives, despite our best intentions and efforts, it's just taken us a little (or a lot) longer to learn how to create the right environment in which our beautiful gardens can grow, and to figure out how to make the bindweed go away - and stay away.

Better late than never. Just plant yourself in your garden on a regular basis, take a look around at the gorgeous plants that you've helped to grow and thrive. Poke around between them and under their leaves, and look for the weeds, whatever you don't want, and get rid of it.

Whatever that means to you - whatever is cluttering up your garden, whatever is spoiling the view, whatever you don't want, get rid of it. And although you'll probably have some bits of bindweed that keep springing up here and there (because Life is like that, there are certain unpleasant bits that we just have to tolerate), at least you can be aware of that and do your best to keep it from destroying the rest of your garden.

13. The journey

The hitchhiker stands at the side of the road, a duffel bag at his feet, backpack slung over his shoulder, an arm extended. At the end of it, his request for a lift appears in the form of his thumb pointing in the direction of his destination. He waits, hopeful. He puts on his most winning smile with the approach of every car, every van, every lorry. The smile slides from his face, dissolving into his slumped shoulders as he sighs and waits for the next one, slightly less hopeful with each vehicle that passes without stopping.

After a while, he picks up his duffel bag, resigned to the fact that he's not getting anywhere and it's time to move on. He knows he'll get tired from walking and carrying his belongings, but he's pretty tired of standing there, too, wasting time, his destination seeming further away than ever.

'Right,' he thinks. 'Let's move on.' Determined to reach his destination, he sets off, humming and whistling now and then, as it's a pretty decent day and all things considered, life is pretty good.

He hears the approach of a vehicle, turns toward it, brings out the winning smile and the accompanying thumb, but again he must keep walking. 'No matter,' he thinks. 'I'll get there. Someone will stop.'

A while later, a truck comes up from behind and slows, eyeing the hopeful hitchhiker suspiciously, and making our traveller peer back equally so. Sizing each other up, and making their decisions, the driver picks up speed without stopping and the hitchhiker is relieved. He trudges along, hoping for better luck next time.

Clouds move in. The wind picks up. The rains come. Our hitc-hiker is not deterred. His situation is unpleasant but what's a little water? Or even a lot? Dejection and discouragement swirl round him, dancing and teasing like naughty little boys who rush forward to poke him, then dart away and laugh. Ignoring them with visions of reaching his destination, he continues to put one soggy foot in front of the other and keeps going.

Cars come. Cars go. The rain falls harder. The temperature drops, and so do the hitchhiker's spirits. Hesitation wraps itself around his weary legs, weighing them down like sandbags of doubt. Thoughts of turning back roll through his mind, each one heavier than the last. It would have been so much easier to not have set out on this journey, to have stayed where he was comfortable.

Comfortable, yes. But not particularly happy.

But would he be any happier when he reached his destination? Of this, he could not be certain. He knew only that he had to discover the answer, whatever it might be. Going back was not an option; there was nothing for him there. Nothing but familiarity and a gnawing, aching emptiness that could no longer be filled by complacency.

A lorry stops. The driver leans across from his seat and opens the passenger door.

"Get in!" he calls to the shivering man. "You must be freezing!"

"You're right, mate, I am! Thanks!" comes the grateful reply as the traveller climbs inside.

The two drive on together, stopping for a greasy burger and chips, some strong, hot coffee around mid-day, before going their separate ways as the lorry driver can take the hitchhiker no further.

With hopes renewed and his belly full, our traveller stands once again at the side of the road, as his thumb and his most winning smile make the silent request for another lift toward his destination...

14. Need a dream? Get one. The Dream Store never closes.

Do you have a dream? Maybe even a few? I hope so. But I know it's possible that you don't.

Perhaps you had one that died. And if that's the case, what happened to it? Did you or someone else kill it? Or did it die from neglect?

It is our natural state to dream. Little kids are always fantasising, dreaming about what they want to be when they grow up. They use their imaginations and make up games all the time. They're creative, inventive, loaded with ideas and possibilities.

Somewhere along the way, after a lot of disillusionment and crushing disappointment, they turned around and saw that their dreams had disappeared. There was no more fantasising. No more believing in possibilities, or even in themselves. Their journeys had become flat, lifeless, boring.

So one pointless step after another, they plod on through life, shoulders drooping, head hanging, wondering why they should bother at all, except to get the bills paid and muddle through the long string of unexciting, uninspiring days that lie ahead.

Insert a dream into that picture, a vision for something wonderful, something fulfilling and rewarding that lies ahead and you get a completely different feeling.

Suddenly, everything has colour again. There is a reason to get through those days. There is excitement, anticipation, planning and hoping. Everything looks brighter because life has meaning and purpose again.

When you have dreams, they'll always be a reflection of some big part of who you are. In pursuing those dreams, you're on a path that leads you to greater self-awareness, self-expression and creativity.

With each new dream you have, you discover even more about yourself. You explore, reach, stretch, and get a little closer to becoming all you're meant to be.

As a hypnotist, I've seen some pretty amazing things that can be achieved in the body because of the power of the mind. So even if you have a dream that you think is impossible, keep dreaming, even if for no other reason than "it feels good." It transports you to a beautiful, happy place, alters the chemistry in your body and lifts your spirits.

We have enough misery in life; it's great to have some fun and be on the lookout for happiness wherever we can find it. So what if you're 68 years old and everyone thinks you're nuts to still dream of being a rock star someday? Put on those leathers, strap on your guitar and scream till you're hoarse, all the while envisioning the sea of faces in front of you, the tens of thousands who have come to hear your music.

Have you forgotten how to dream? I've been there - more than once. For most of my life, every dream I ever had was blown to smithereens so I gave up bothering after a while. I went so long without having one, I didn't even think about them any more.

But then I changed my life. And suddenly, dreams began to spring up again out of nowhere. Now I'm actively digging for them and I've got so many, I can't keep track. They motivate me, inspire me, encourage me as I'm motoring along through my insanely busy life. They are the reason I work crazy hours and have my hand in so many pots, I've lost count.

My days revolve around pursuing my dreams, which makes me happier than I could ever begin to describe. I'm truly blessed in that everything I do for "work" is just a natural part of who I am, so it doesn't feel like work. I'm just living somewhere on the continuum of my dreams which have been realised to a great extent in some ways, but not in others - yet - and I look forward to watching them unfold.

Having been dreamless for such a long time, it makes me even more appreciative for the many dreams I have now, especially as I'm seeing them become my reality. I don't even care about the ones that died or were beaten to death so long ago.

I wish that at those times, I'd have seen that I just needed to get a new one. I wouldn't have suffered so much, wouldn't have felt that terrible aching loss and emptiness that goes with grieving for something that never will be.

But that was before I knew any better.

I don't want to hear about how it hurts to dream and have it be taken from you. Stop dwelling on the past. Just because previous dreams were shattered, it doesn't mean the next one will be, too. And if it is, you'll survive.

If you don't have a dream right now, get one. You can go to the Dream Store. It never closes. There's an endless selection of dreams, in every shape, colour and magnitude imaginable. And guess what? They're free. They let you take as many as you want. They don't even care if you stuff your pockets with them, only to take them home and stash them away for later.

Okay. Now you know there's no excuse for not having a dream. If you don't have one, do yourself a really enormous favour *today*, before you go to bed tonight.

Go on now. Get yourself a dream.

15. Words.

Words. Words, words, words. There are too many. There are not enough. There are too many wrong ones.

They cause too much trouble, words do. If you use too many, you may be in trouble. If you don't use enough, you may be in trouble. If you do not use the right ones, or if you don't use them in the correct order, you may be in trouble.

I have wasted far too many words in this life. They have been very expensive; there has been a terrible cost. It has taken me many years to discover the true value in words, and to understand that "less is more". They are so powerful and so precious! I want to use only my best words. And sometimes I want to use none.

I am a communicator. I have always been a communicator. Although half of communication is about listening, people have come to expect me to do much of the talking. They want me to talk when they do not wish to do it themselves. And they want me to listen when they need an ear. I love listening. I would rather listen than speak much of the time. I want to speak only when I have something to say, and not because it is required of me to ease the discomfort of others who do not wish to speak themselves.

But when the only way I wish to communicate is by listening and others want me to be talking, they think something is wrong. They think I'm upset. They think I'm not well.

When really, I'm just tired of stringing words together in my head and making them come out of my mouth because someone else requires, expects, or just wants that from me.

Sometimes I want to be The Quiet One. Sometimes I want to be the one who just gets to sit and listen. Sometimes I am tired of being the one who is supposed to carry the conversation and I just want to sit back and observe, digest, absorb, take in.

But people do not like it when I take on this role. Many times, when I've been with people who are quiet and I stop speaking, the conversation stops right along with me. It becomes awkward. There are horrible, long silences.

I wait. I hope. I pray that someone else will offer a topic and begin discussions. More often than not, it does not happen.

And to rid everyone present of the dreadful uncomfortableness, eventually I will speak, yet again. And I will go home feeling like I said too much, yet again. I will have left them all feeling relieved because there was someone else to take up the awkward, empty silences that they did not want to fill.

I do not always want to risk having said too much, or not having used the right words. It is easier to be The Quiet One. I want only the responsibility of listening, and I want to do it well. If I do not get to remain quiet a good deal of the time, how will I learn? How will I digest and absorb, or grow? How will I find out who you are and what is important to you?

Even a teapot gets to refilled before it is pouring, pouring, pouring once again.

Words. Words, words, words. There are right ones and there are wrong ones. And most often, the wrong ones are only wrong because of the filter through which they were heard by another. Your choice of words may have been quite right, and only innocuous. But heard through the filter of someone else's own pain and experience, they become pure acid.

And you meant no harm at all. But there it is. The damage is done. You may or may not be given an opportunity to explain. And the explanation may or may not be accepted.

And if not, then the damage is permanent.

Words. They are so delicious. You can serve them up like whipped cream on a dessert, but it's what's under them that matters. You can keep them light and simple, like jiggling, red, sparkling Jell-O. Or they can be heavy, complex, a seven-layer chocolate torte filled with nuts, fruit, and a silky smooth ganache.

Sometimes people have no idea there is a torte hiding under that yummy whipped topping, and they think there is only Jell-O. I cannot be upset with those who do not like or understand - or even recognise - a seven-layer torte. Those people are simply not good at desserts; it is not their fault.

Sometimes people insist upon digging through my Jell-O words, certain that there is layer after layer of complicated meaning, refusing to accept that not everything needs analysis, complexity or a connection with the Divine Source of All. I do not appreciate it when my simple but pretty, jiggling, red Jell-O is torn up with the fork of someone who is frantically searching for several layers of cake, ganache, nuts and fruit.

And all the while, wasting far too many words to do it.

Throughout my life, I have often wondered what it would be like if we were only allotted a certain number of syllables to use, and what would happen if suddenly, mid-sentence - mid-word - you used up your last syllable and that was it, no more could come out of your mouth.

Similarly, if you were writing, and came to the end of your allowed number of words and that was it, no more letters could be formed by pen or computer. Like permanent writer's block.

Is this what happened to people who are no longer able to communicate? Have they used up their allowed syllables?

My syllables are very precious to me. I've wasted so many; I don't want to waste any more. I need to be a teapot. I am a teapot, whether or not other people would prefer it if I were a waterfall.

Words cut and divide. They mend and heal. They hurt and destroy. They inspire and stimulate. They kill and maim. They nurture and encourage. They are poison and medicine.

16. The Magician's Secrets.

Yesterday, I had occasion to do some healing on someone who was in pain. And as usual, when I finished 'doing my thing' a few minutes later, she felt much better.

It's about 18 years ago now since the first time I did it, with only some quiet words inside me, telling me what to do and how to do it when I was sitting next to a man who was in pain. I had no idea what I was doing but did it anyway, and after a few moments, his pain was gone.

Needless to say, we were both shocked. And over the years since that incredible night, I've seen some pretty cool things happen as a result of doing this healing on people.

Every now and then, I see people I healed many years ago and am told that they're still pain-free after I "zapped" away long-term suffering

The first time I ever did this publicly, I was astonished by the crowd that showed up. I was going to do some healing in the back room of a little village pub - and the whole bar was packed, standing room only.

And they were all there to see me. Here? In the Midlands? In this very rural little village?? Go figure.

Unfortunately, I couldn't get to everyone, but I did 6 hours of back-to-back healing on about 30 people. I shocked and converted the hecklers who could not believe the troubles and ailments I "knew", that I could determine exactly where they hurt and how it felt - and they couldn't believe they felt better by the time they went home.

Just like magic.

As a psychic and a medium, I did readings for years before taking to the stage to connect audience members with loved ones in spirit. I've seen the powerful healing and comfort that come from being able to link energies here with energies 'on the other side'. I'm like Mrs. Olson plugging things into the switchboard, connecting people on the phone on Little House on the Prairie (or Little Prairie Under The House, as I like to call it) and listening in on the conversations.

It's always been such a moving thing to see the bittersweet tears that come from someone who is in communication with a loved one in spirit. I tell them things I wouldn't otherwise know, things that make no sense to me, but I see the recognition and understanding on their faces. It makes me so happy to know that they're comforted by the messages given to them. Sometimes there is laughter, an apology or forgiveness, permission to move on with their lives. But always, that connection is very healing and powerful.

Just like magic.

I've been asked many times throughout my life about my abilities as a psychic, a medium and a healer. How do I know this, how do I do that, how does this work?

The truth is, I don't know. And I don't want to know.

I know only one thing about it for sure: It does work.

It's really no different from wondering how you get flowers or vegetables or mighty oak trees by planting something in the ground. Or how you start with two tiny cells and end up with an actual person. Or how your body knows how to do this or that, creating chemicals and hormones that do certain jobs. Or how all those systems function, how organs know what to do.

Scientists cannot really explain any of that. They like to think they can because they tell you what happens. But they don't actually tell you how it happens. Whatever that 'thing' is that makes an actual person appear with all the right parts in the right places, doing what they're meant to do, whatever it is that makes that little seed start to grow and sprout and produce big juicy strawberries - we do not know how this happens.

But if we knew how those seeds grow, if we knew how those little cells become an actual person, if we understood a healer's seemingly miraculous ability to cure, or the link between the spirit and earthly realms, it would be like watching David Copperfield's "magic acts" and having the answers to "how does he do that?" Do you really want to know?

I wish guys like that hadn't started calling themselves "illusionists." I liked it better when they were "magicians." To tell me it's an illusion is admitting that I'm seeing something that isn't real. It's like acknowledging this is all just an act, a trick.

Miracles, the unexplained, the great mysteries of life are what add a beautiful sense of wonder to our lives. Just look at the delight and sense of awe on the face of a child who sees presents from Father Christmas left under the tree! Wow, he was actually **there**?? And look! The milk and cookies that were left for him are **gone**! Just watch little kids at a "magic show", seeing tricks that as adults, we understand. Their eyes as big as saucers, jaws in their little laps, their astonishment and amazement are truly wonderful.

But when we grow up, we know the truth about Father Christmas. And we know about all the stuff that's up that magician's sleeves. We lose that sense of wonder as we grow and learn about the world and the magic disappears.

Not understanding how things grow or how healers heal or how a medium links us to spirit is just the way it should be. It's like the Universe's gift to us, a gift that allows us to retain a sense of childlike wonder about the great mysteries of life.

I don't know about you, but I don't want to know the answers. I'd rather believe in magic.

17. Delicious bits

The smell of freshly mown grass. Or lilacs, roses or freesia. Or my favourite - star-gazer lilies. Their powerful scent is intoxicating and fills a room for several days.

Bread baking, or a spice cake full of ginger, cinnamon and cloves. Or rich chocolate brownies, warm and gooey just out of the oven.

A slice of lemon - oh, and eating the whole thing like an orange... yummmm... I know, it's not for everyone but my mouth waters every time I think of it. I love sour but am not keen on sweet except in small doses now and then.

Crisp, just barely ripe Macintosh or Granny Smith apples - oh, my... how I love them but they do not love me so I cannot eat them. But I do still love that delightfully fresh scent.

The crackling of a fire, quietly glowing and warming those near enough to enjoy its hypnotic dance. The silent drifting of huge, fat, fluffy flakes of snow, falling softly against a moonlit backdrop of winter.

The soft and sweet warmth of a little scrap of life in the form of a kitty, curled up and sleeping on my lap or nestled against my chest as I lie on my side...I miss this more than many things; it is not possible for me to have a kitty right now but my neighbours' cats come to visit and let me pretend that they're mine.

Being curled up under a thick duvet in a darkened room, early in the morning and listening to the soft, steady sound of a summer rain lullaby. Pulling the duvet up a little higher, snuggling down a little deeper, knowing you can lie there as long as you want and listen to the sweet music outside...

Gazing at water, a lake with swans and geese gliding across it like tiny feathered sailboats. Watch them long enough and you become transfixed. Or an ocean, with beautiful waves gently rolling toward the shore, one after another, their rhythmic splashing against the sand the sweetest music you've ever heard.

The feel of your sleeping child's even breath kissing your neck as you hold that little person close, stroking silky soft hair and so filled with love you think you'll burst.

Warm sun on my skin, gentle, like a hug from the universe. Cheery little birds, going about their bird business as they chat and sing amongst themselves, decorating the air with pretty notes that drift and float.

The sounds of certain words, especially Italian or Spanish words. They can make even the nastiest thing sound romantic, erotic, sensuous.

Music. Sweet, sweet music.... found in words of love or the most tender caresses. Laughter, blissful smiles, a joyful heart singing a crystal clear, sparkling melody.

Hugs. Wonderful, squooshy, celebratory, passionate, warm, consoling, excited, I hurt more than I can stand it, I love you more than you know, I'm so happy to meet you, delicious hugs, hugs for every occasion, create an occasion to have a hug, have several and enjoy every perfect moment and let them heal your wounded soul.

Berries. Mmm, berries. Big, juicy strawberries, so sweet, and raspberries, or plump and perky little blueberries, bursting in your mouth.

Water. Fresh, beautiful clear water, icy cold, life-giving, rejuvenating as it slides down your parched throat on a busy day, a dry day, a hot day - just any day.

Water. Hot, steaming, bubbling and scented as you slide your weary body into a huge tub and soak away all your troubles, your stresses, your aches and your pains. Thinking only of how wonderful it feels to lie there, in quiet candlelight as you rest a while.

Waking up and having been given another day. A glorious gift. Too precious for words. And the best way to acknowledge that gift is to spend as much of it in enjoyment and awareness of life's beauty and magic as you can manage.

They're everywhere. All you have to do is notice.

18. The healing power of Friendship

Once upon a time, there was a tiny acorn, who lived in a remote brown valley.

She was a very sad little acorn because there was always fighting there, and black soupy clouds that hung low and heavy like soot which made it difficult for her to breathe.

The little acorn hated it there and was desperate to escape. But as she looked around, she could see nothing but hills.

'Oh, dear!' she thought. 'The only way out of here is to roll uphill! I don't think I can do it!'

But it was either that or stay in the dark and toxic valley where nothing grew and nothing could breathe.

So the little acorn made the arduous journey uphill, where she came to rest in a lovely, sunny spot.

Over many years, she grew into a grand old oak tree. There were no other oak trees up there because no other acorns had been brave enough to make the journey up that hill. If not for the little birds who nested and sang amongst her beautiful branches, and the squirrels who ran up and down her sturdy trunk, chattering and chasing each other on a summer's day, the oak tree would not have had any company at all.

The oak tree could not help but envy her little friends. They had all the freedom in the world, while she was firmly rooted to the ground and could not move from that spot. Smiling a sad and wistful smile, she watched in silence as the squirrels darted here and there, playing hide and seek, and the birds flew in and out of her branches, chirping and singing their sweet songs of freedom.

Her little friends felt her sadness, but no matter what they did, nothing cheered her. She would not play with them. She would not speak to them. She just wished she could be them.

Unbeknownst to the oak tree, there was a horrible black disease growing deep within her trunk. It had been there, lying in wait, since she was a tiny acorn choking on the heavy sooty air of the valley below. After many years, it was finally cutting off the tree's supply of food and water. Her pretty leaves began to turn yellow and fall to the ground. Her branches began to dry up, and tiny twigs snapped at the slightest touch. Little holes appeared in her trunk, as the black disease ate its way to the outside world.

Fearing the worst and not wanting to upset her little friends, she said not a word. There was nothing she could do, nowhere she could go. Unlike the birds and squirrels, she was stuck well and truly into the ground with no freedom to move. All she could do was pray silently that one day, she would be well again.

But of course, her friends could see that something was wrong, even though the tree smiled bravely and insisted that she was fine.

Eventually ignoring the tree, a very colourful but somewhat bossy bird took it upon herself to fly to the home of a wizard who lived some distance away.

After relating the tree's story, the bird begged, "Please, would you help my beautiful friend?"

"Of course I will," the wizard replied. Hastily, he scrawled on a scrap of paper and handed it to the bossy bird. "Gather these ingredients and put them in the holes in her trunk. And soon, she will be healed completely."

The bird put the list in her beak and flew back to her friends. Everyone was excited to learn that their lovely friend would be well if they could just get everything on that list. After a discussion about where to find the ingredients, the birds flew off to the furthest places and the squirrels scampered up and down the hills nearer their home.

When all of them met up again, they had collected an abundance of exactly what the wizard prescribed. Specific bits of berries and bark, leaves and moss lay beneath her boughs, sweet medicine brought by her friends. And they brought even more birds and squirrels back with them, along with some bunnies and chipmunks, and some other new friends.

Following the wizard's instructions, the squirrels ran up and down the trunk, filling every hole with the herbal concoction that would kill every bit of the black disease and bring strength and healing to the beautiful tree.

When they were finished, all the birds and animals gathered on the ground in a huge circle around the tree. As per the wizard's instructions, they huddled together and envisioned her being strong and well. They prayed for her healing. Old friends and new, they wished the Black Disease would be gone.

Suddenly, the holes began to close. The twigs were green again. New leaves were budding and sprouting and the lovely old oak tree was even grander and more beautiful than before. Never had she felt so well in her life. Everything looked bigger, brighter, and more wonderful.

And when her little friends played in her branches, scampered up and down her trunk or played at her feet, she laughed and smiled along with them, teasing and giggling and being a part of their games for many long years.

And she was never lonely again.

19. Addiction was my master. And now it is my slave.

Tormented, I ripped myself away from my vile lover years ago, tearing off chunks of my flesh as though it were frozen to metal. His powerful hands have left prints on my body, his seductive kisses are burned into my soul where he skulks in the darkest shadows.

He waits, knowing, trusting that I will once again be tempted, that I will return to him and give myself to him completely. And he is right. I am tempted. I am often tempted. I ache for him, my man in black. I close my eyes, recalling the sweet delight in his deadly touch. My skin comes alive, aching as his masterful fingers caress me from a distant time, from yesterday, from a hundred years from now. I will never be free.

A tiny voice inside pleads with him to stop but a much louder one begs him to go on, to entice me, persuade me, to seduce me yet again. And he knows this. He always knows this because that voice is his. He hears my every thought, his sadistic laughter echoing through my heart as it loves and hates him, needs and despises him, craves and rejects him all at once.

Ever the trickster, sometimes he lets me think he is out of my head, that I am free at last. He deceives me, leaves me alone. Allows me to forget him, at least for a little while. Just long enough for me to let down my guard. Just long enough for me to get comfortable, to stop noticing the scars, to stop the deadly dance that's in my brain, and I think perhaps I am finally safe.

But I am not. Time and time again, I discover that he is lurking in the shadows, waiting until I am at my most vulnerable. Like a shark detecting a few drops of blood from miles away, there he is, silently gliding through the darkest waters of my soul, anticipating his victory over my crumbling will.

I am, however, intimately familiar with this game. He thrives on my power;

he feeds on my will. I love to be at his mercy and I hate it, detest it, loathe it yet I fantasize about my submission, about giving myself to him completely, crossing back over to the dark side once again.

Everything in this twisted game is about power, about control; ever the masochist, I take sadistic pleasure in my own suffering. It empowers me. The longer I endure it, the stronger I become.

My most vulnerable weakness is my greatest strength and he does not understand this. He has not learned that I am using him as he has always used me. His strength becomes my own and I use it against him, every time those jaws come up from the very depths of my being and try to swallow me whole.

He does not understand that he is only as powerful as he ever was, but that my own strength increases every time I am able to pull myself away from the seductive dance, the lie that tells me "Just this once will be okay", the lame excuse that tries to twist itself into a justifiable reason, that makes his deadly grasp a loving embrace.

My sadistic lover is addiction and I am its Master. I fight the slavery of submission as much as I crave its sweet poison. On days like this, at moments like this, I find it impossible to imagine having gone for very long periods without noticing the chains of addiction wrapping themselves around me so tightly I could not move, could not breathe.

But this is because the chains don't always look the same. My sadistic lover is always there, in one form or another, and I must be ever vigilant, never letting my guard down, watching for that moment when I lose control and slide into self-destruction yet again. I will not be defeated. I will continue to fight and continue to win.

And I will continue to delight in my sadistic lover's seductive and terrifying enticement. It is delicious and decadent; it is sensuous and erotic. It awakens me and stirs something deep within me, bringing me to life while it seeks my destruction.

I delight in all this terrible passion yet I will not succumb. It flirts, it teases me, taunts and dares me. But it is only a game in my head, where I am both Master and Slave. I use it to my own advantage, for self-discipline and strength. I toy with it now, as it used to toy with me.

No, I do not want freedom from this addiction because it feeds my strength, my willpower, my ability to turn my back on its gripping temptation and refuse to give in.

I can look at my sadistic addiction with passion or disdain; it is my choosing. And even when it is with erotic pleasure, I can enjoy the dance but say goodnight at the door.

And so, in this moment, as in so many other moments and days, even months and years before it, I will.

20. Patience ain't so virtuous after all.

Impatience. I've been really good at it in my life. I'll tell you, five children certainly killed a lot of it though. You just have to slow down to Kid Speed when you're trying to get ready to go somewhere, do anything...life becomes One Big Long Wait.

But even then, I still had that streak, that 'something' that made me want to hurry up and get things done, or have something happen. I used to plead with the universe to give me more patience, going way back to when I was in my late teens and early 20s with just one or two children. "Please give me patience!" rolled through my mind and off my tongue on a regular basis.

A few more kids and a career as a homeopath later, it occurred to me that the universe had answered my prayers by giving me "patients" - and lots of them...

I suppose somewhere along the way, I had also got the other kind, too, but I've still got a little kid trying to hide just below the surface (but she does it badly) and I get extremely impatient about exciting things happening, or when I wish something unpleasant would just hurry up and be finished.

I'm not so sure impatience is always a bad thing, although to hear most people talk about it, it is. Like everything, it has pros and cons. And frankly, so does patience. It's not always such a great thing and I don't know why it's "a virtue." I can think of a lot of things that are far more virtuous than that, but why didn't they rate getting their own 'common expression' when they're far more deserving of it?

It's true, being patient feels a lot better than being impatient. There's something to be said for being quite content to just be where you are, doing what you're doing, not freaking out or anxious or eager or restless or fidgeting or jiggling or pacing about something you wish would hurry up and happen. That 'about to climb out of your skin' feeling is not pleasant.

And that 'Oh, **no**, what have I **done**?' feeling sucks even worse when you've rushed into something you're gonna regret - like, for example, a bad tattoo or an even worse marriage. Heaven knows I dashed up the proverbial aisle so fast a time or two, I caused a draft. I've had baths that lasted longer than a couple of my engagements. And brushing my teeth has taken longer than a couple of my courtships, too.

At least my tattoos are all fab, even though I got a few of them pretty quickly. And unlike marriage (at least for me), they'll last forever and I'd happily get more. One day I might actually end up with as many tattoos as I've had marriages.

I remember wanting to buy a particular house which was absolutely adorable and had a lot going for it. I thought the asking price was reasonable and was happy to offer it. I SO loved that house, I wanted my estate agent to hurry up and make the offer right away! - but he insisted on going through every one of his painstakingly careful lists of comparisons and evaluations.

I kept pleading with him to just offer the asking price, feeling a terrible sense of urgency, afraid I'd lose this adorable little house.

"Relax!" he said. "It's been on the market for a while and no one's showed any interest."

So I fidgeted and sighed and paced and tried not to gnaw off my fingers for the next few hours as my insanely patient estate agent took his time coming up with what he thought was a reasonable offer, and one that quite frankly, I thought was embarrassing.

By the time he rang the seller's agent later that day, out of the blue two other offers had been made, both of which were higher than the one my agent wanted me to make - and both were below the asking price. Had I done what I thought was right, and as quickly as I wanted to do it, I'd have had the house. My impatience would have served me well. And listening to that little voice inside would have made all the difference.

And more often than not, with dates set and guests invited, I knew I shouldn't have been going through with those most of my weddings. Speedy or not, when things felt really wrong, I should have listened to my guts and backed out.

But instead, I succumbed to pressure or ultimatums or worries about hurting someone. I figured I had cold feet, that it would all be okay, and I swore that no matter what, I would make it work.

My tattoos felt really right, and they're great and I love them. That adorable little house, and the price I wanted to offer felt really right, too. I was gutted when it didn't work out.

And when that little voice was screaming at me not to go through with all those weddings, I should have listened. My impatience may have made me say yes to That Burning Question or set a date that was five minutes away (although I'd like to say it was just my idealistic and very romantic nature). But impatience wasn't what made me ignore what I knew was the right thing to do.

As those weddings approached and I knew they were as wrong as wrong could be, I shouldn't have worried about everyone else's feelings, or what they wanted, needed or expected from me.

My soap-opera life has taught me very many lessons, one of which is that impatience, in and of itself, is not necessarily a bad thing. Nor is patience always so virtuous. In fact, sometimes it causes more harm than good when you wait too long because of a fear, a worry, a doubt about something, and you miss a miraculous moment or a fantastic opportunity.

If I've learned nothing else in the insanity that has been my life, it is to listen to my guts. To follow my instincts.

Now, if I'm feeling impatient, I just make extra sure I check in with the little voice. I've discovered that my motivation for the impatience is what is significant and it makes all the difference between a bad decision and a good one.

And when I'm feeling patient to the point of reluctance, I check in about that, too, so I can work out if there's some fear or another issue holding me back.

The most important bit is to listen to that little voice because it is Pure Wisdom and it'll never steer you wrong.

21. Family. Is there a more emotionally-charged word?

The free "prize" that goes with purchases usually looks okay on the surface. And it'll usually serve its purpose in a pretty basic way. You might find yourself wishing it was the model with this option or that one, a few bells and whistles, and boy, if you could have chosen which one you wanted in that line, it would have been one of the upgraded versions.

You eye that nicer model somewhat wistfully, thinking "Mmmmm, I wish......." and going over the list of options that are so appealing. It does **this** and it does **that**, and then it does **this**, too! Wow... yours only does this and that.

"Ah, well. It works," you tell yourself in an attempt to feel satisfied with what you were given.

We slide out of the universe, landing straight into a pile of people who are pretty much your standard issue family. Maybe a bell and a whistle, perhaps a few extra options, and most of them have some cracks, dents or broken bits. They still work but for the most part, they are not the upgraded versions that you'd really love to have.

Many of them will be in your face, jamming their noses into your business with every other heartbeat. Some of them might not give a rat's @$$ what you do - or don't do.

Your mother may drive you absolutely mental. She calls it love and nurturing. You call it suffocating and neurotic.

Your sister steals your make-up, your clothes, your boyfriend. You want to chuck her off a bridge but you don't realise that she admires you, looks up to you, wants to be just like you.

You might have landed in a blended family, or one that is missing various members, probably for a variety of very painful reasons. Perhaps it's an extremely toxic family and it makes you sick right through to your soul.

But whatever it is, warts, poisons, neuroses and all, it's your family. And you might well be wishing you had one of the upgraded versions you've seen in other people's homes.

In a way, you can have one of those models. You can do a sort of Mr Potato-head thing, taking several parts and putting them together to create your Potato-family. This can help to heal the parts of your own that are missing, broken, dented or damaged.

I was given a bunch of mothers in this life (in an assortment of birth, foster and adopted). Yet I never knew what it was to feel "mothered". This caused me a lot of pain for a very long time and my agonising attempts to win that motherly love I craved were utterly futile and self-destructive.

But I've had the extremely good fortune to be given lots of mother-substitutes throughout my life, women who were very maternal, nurturing, soothing and comforting. They gave me a taste of what it's like to be mothered and it's really delicious. Many times, I've been moved to tears by the ease with which these women offered their beautiful mothering gift to me - one in particular, a tiny, lovely woman with the biggest, most nurturing and maternal heart I'd ever been blessed to know.

As for my adopted family, my parents are both dead and I have no relationship with anyone else, apart from a beautiful aunt and occasionally a cousin.

Luckily, I have some very loving birth family members in my life, an aunt, a cousin, a brother and sister, a niece and nephew, and there a few others in the background with whom I hope to develop relationships someday.

Then there are a bunch of informally adopted family members, my 'Mum', sisters, a brother or two. There were even a couple of grandparents thrown into the mix, too, a long time ago but they died some years back.

There have been so many wonderful people with whom I've shared loving connections and bonds that have felt more like family than most of the people to whom I've been related by blood or by law. The beauty of these family members is they don't offer the same kinds of dysfunctional, enmeshed, crazy-making interference and emotional upsets that "traditional" families do. Bonus!

"Family" most certainly does not have to mean the prize that comes with the purchase, although some of those basic models are quite good and if you're one of the lucky ones who is happy with yours, I'm thrilled that you were so blessed - and no doubt you are thrilled, too.

And if you weren't one of those people, if the word "family" conjures up pain and heartache, or loneliness and emptiness, I hope you've been able to create your own upgraded model, adding the bells and whistles, choosing specific options that allow you to feel loved and supported, welcomed and valued, the way a real family is intended to be.

It doesn't matter what shape or size it is, or where it comes from, or how you stumbled into it, as long as you have a group of people in your life who feel like your family in all the best ways.

22. Ambition.

"Don't go out with that guy. He's got no ambition. He'll never amount to anything," says the Daddy to his all-grown-up 'little girl'. "You'll never have anything. Do you want a nice house like this? Do you want a nice car? You've always enjoyed the extras in life, thanks to my hard work. Do you want to throw it all away on some guy who has no ambition?"

It's another day and another guy. Same Daddy. Same all-grown-up 'little girl'.

"I don't trust him," says the Daddy. "He's awfully ambitious. I think he'd sell his own mother to get to the top of the company. He's always thinking of the next promotion, always angling for a way to be recognised by the boss. Did you see that house of his? And he drives a Mercedes? He's too young to have all that! Nope, I don't trust him. He's too ambitious."

Okay, so which is it? Do we like ambition or not? It's a word that wears two different coats, and it's only your perspective that changes it from one to the other. All it takes is a smile on your face and in your voice to make it a really wonderful quality. Or it takes a slight squint and a little sneer to turn it into a greedy, selfish, heartless thing.

Here are some more Matthew Good lyrics for you, from one of his coolest songs, "21st Century Living":

"Ambition, ambition's a tricky thing, it's like riding a unicycle over a dental floss tightrope, over a wilderness of razor blades."

Wow. That's quite a powerful image. But is he right about that?

Certainly, we need some ambition in life. It's what pushes us forward to chase our dreams, reach our goals. It's what urges us to be educated, to make a good living (whatever that means to each of us individually). Without it, we'd be in trouble. Without it, our dreams would die. We may not even bother to have any in the first place.

But can you have too much ambition? I suppose the short answer is "yes", although in reality, I don't believe that in those cases, ambition is the problem. "Yes" if Daddy is right about someone selling his own mother to get ahead.

But you know what? Ambition is not that man's problem. And that's assuming that Daddy is right about the man. Perhaps Daddy's the one with the problem, being jealous, envious, wishing he had what the man has, wishing he had been as successful in his career as the man was, wishing he'd chased his dreams rather than giving them up.

In and of itself, there is nothing wrong with wanting to achieve great things and/or earn a lot of money - tons of it, if you want it. Look at Oprah, for example. She has accomplished astonishing things. And she's worth billions but she is just as down-to-earth, as kind, as "real" as your next-door neighbour.

In those cases where we say someone's ambition is a negative thing, it's not really ambition that's the problem. It's fear. And it drives insecurity, jealousy, greed and selfishness. Perhaps it's a fear of not being good enough. A fear of poverty or not having enough. Fear of disappointing someone. Fear of rejection.

I understand what Matthew Good is talking about. He means 'ambition' the same way Daddy does, the way many people do. He means that we can go too far in the pursuit of success, but that's not about ambition.

Daddy knows ambition is a good thing or he wouldn't be telling his little girl to stay away from men who don't seem to have any. He knows it is essential to fulfillment and happiness, to achieving goals and making dreams come true.

But Daddy operates out of fear and does not understand that ambition is not the same as greed, disrespect, manipulation, trampling others while you get what you want or need.

Yeah, ambition is a good thing.

23. Crank that wheel away from the skid.

You know that heart-stopping fear that fills you with ice water when you're driving along, and suddenly you find yourself in a skid? Your car fish-tails back and forth, back and forth, spitting gravel or spinning on ice and visions of a rather messy and imminent death race through your mind.

Your stomach flips as adrenalin floods your taut body. You grip the wheel in white-knuckled terror, and is your mouth really filled with cotton balls all of a sudden?

Those seconds hang like years, and you're sure you've lost a few off your life after this too-close call that leaves you shaken and trembling at the side of the road.

Growing up in Western Canada where the weather can be brutal and extreme, I learned how to drive in some pretty vicious conditions. There's nothing like plowing through tons of snow on several inches of solid ice, with a raging snowstorm obscuring your vision - by night.

And unlike here in England, many of Canada's country roads are gravel, which can send you into a nasty skid and land you in the ditch in as big a hurry as that ice under your wheels will do.

What makes it worse is the instinct that some people have to crank the steering wheel into the direction of the skid. A big no-no. And on top of that, some people find themselves staring at whatever they're trying to avoid. Another vehicle, a wall, a sharp embankment that drops off and will send them plummeting below and into a raging river.

I came out of the chute in the middle of a sharp skid, born to a frightened young teen and after a time was taken from her and adopted into yet another skid. Much of my life was spent fish-tailing back and forth, back and forth, every heart-stopping moment spent cranking the wheel hard in the opposite direction of that skid, and doing my best to stay focused on the road, and not on the ditch, the wall - or many times, the cliff above the river.

I was not always successful. In fact, I was very unsuccessful on far too many occasions for far too many years.

With the passage of time and continued practice and focus, the skids are now a lot fewer and farther in between. They don't usually land me in the ditch any more either, because I've learned to stay focused on the road.

And if you don't already know how to do it, you can learn, too.

24. Life and a stone butterfly.

I've always loved my bedroom in this quirky old cottage. With its sloped ceilings on the front and back walls, its big thick beams, old-fashioned cream-coloured wallpaper that was just so "me" with its tiny blue flowers, and the 500-year-old original oak flooring made with huge, wide planks, it was comfortable and cosy, a peaceful retreat from the first moment it was mine. Sparsely decorated with antiques and old-style lamps, it was simple and rustic - just as I wanted it.

I loved it exactly the way it was. But a while ago, a bit of that very old and very pretty wallpaper had begun to peel due to water damage after a flood some time ago. Every attempt to re-glue that small strip of paper had failed. The problem only got worse each time.

Clearly, the wallpaper needed removing and the room would need to be painted. I didn't want to face it; this was a change I did not want. But push had come to shove and really, I had no choice.

Ideally, if that perfect wallpaper had to go, I'd have loved to tear out the plaster altogether and restore the stone walls, as a former husband and I had done to two other rooms in this cottage. But for a variety of reasons, it was not on the List of Things To Do at that time.

I guess the Universe had other plans. Once the wallpaper was peeled off, it was discovered that the rain had saturated the daub (a mixture of mud, straw, horse hair and animal dung) that had been used to hold the stones together. Therefore, the plaster had been softening and quietly crumbling without my knowledge. It had to come off.

And if it was going to come off where the damage was, we might as well remove it from all the stone walls in my room and do the repointing.

What had begun as a simple decorating job had suddenly become the restoration of 500-year-old, two-foot-thick stone walls.

I adore doing projects like this, as filthy as they are, and as much as my not-20-years-old-any-more body rebels against the physical labour required. Give me some DIY jobs and I'm as happy as a little kid on Christmas morning.

But a dear friend had arrived from Canada just two days earlier. We were meant to be playing and having fun. Lucky for me, my friend is a good sport and has jumped in to help. (I think the word 'sport' is a contraction for 'support').

For the past several days, I've been chiseling away at the exposed daub, eating clouds of dust from smashed up plaster, rubble and very old mud. And my friend has been right there beside me, chiseling away, too. Inch by inch, chunk by chunk, the daub has been chipped off, dug out, and falling to the floor.

We speak a little now and then, but mostly, each of us is focused on the task at hand: digging out that ancient mud, straw and animal dung, formerly the best binding and reinforcing substance available for constructing a building. Digging it out is a dirty, dusty, filthy job, but it has to be done.

Slowly and steadily, we've been making progress, albeit with hammers occasionally missing their targets, sliding off the chisels and hitting our hands. Knuckles graze against stone, leaving tiny pieces of flesh behind. But we carry on, each with our own sections to do, but jointly working at the completion of one project.

Every now and then, we discover loose stones that require removal. As we pull them out, there is a seemingly endless mountain of dirt, twigs, straw and rubble that just keeps pouring out of the holes. We keep digging, and this nasty stuff just keeps coming.

Horrified to see the gaping holes in front of us, the mountain of dirt at our feet, I sigh, not liking this bigger problem, but knowing that somehow, I will be able to shift some stones and rebuild the whole area. Just as I've done many times before in our other restored rooms. It will just take time and patience.

The digging isn't all bad. I've found some pretty cool stuff in these walls, little treasures that have been delightful discoveries. Some very old coins, wonderful handmade nails, even an unusual ring that just happens to fit me perfectly.

And then there are the stones themselves...their quiet strength, enduring, indefatigable, beautiful, their healing energy spilling forth, permeating my aching spirit. They are just like my friend, who sits beside me here, digging the mud and straw out from between the stones, then stuffing in the mix of sand, stone, lime and cement.

The really messy bit is yet to come. That will be today when we have to bring a hose in from outside and wash down the walls. It creates a sandy, muddy, filthy mess that requires the utmost care with a tarp and loads of towels so as not to have it seep through the numerous cracks in the floor (when it is dark in my bedroom, you can see the light in the parlour below, through those cracks).

My friend will be here for that, too, for the huge mess I'm facing today. Other friends have been pitching in with this project, too. The smashing-up of my pretty bedroom, the 'very much worse before it gets better' renovation and restoration - like so many other things in life, it has been a nasty job, but one that had to be done.

And having faced the deeper problem, the one that lay deep within the walls, having confronted it head-on whether I liked it or not, with my friend at my side, it is being resolved. The walls are much stronger now, and my bedroom will be far more rustic and beautiful than it was with the pretty, old-fashioned wallpaper. I've left or created several holes and little 'shelves' in the walls for ornaments, books, or candles, as I did in the other two rooms, making it truly unique, interesting and romantic.

I will miss my pretty wallpaper, but there has been great - and necessary - transformation within these walls and in my bedroom. For all this work and effort, which included the wonderful help of my good sport friends, I can only look forward to enjoying my beautiful stone butterfly.

25. What I meant was...

Was that post really about my bedroom? Well, yes, every word I said about the room and the project was the truth. But the point was not about the decorating.

Perhaps I am too 'thinky' for my own good. Actually, I know I am. It was kind of funny when a few years ago, someone pointed out how analytical I am.

I thought it was hilarious, in fact. I suppose it struck me as ridiculous because of my interpretation of that word. It reminds me of a man sitting at a desk - or if I have to stretch myself to imagine that it is a woman, her hair is knotted into a tight bun at the back of her head (either that, or it's just very short and unfeminine). And of course, there is a very plain business suit in this picture.

I see calculators and pursed lips and seriousness. Numbers, lines, graphs, statistics. No emotion. No smiles. No warmth.

Nope, none of that fits me. Not at all.

But on thinking about it, as I've done many times since being told this about myself, I had to realise that it's the truth. I am extremely analytical. I think about why and how and where and what. I want to know how things work and especially when we're talking about people.

What makes them tick? Why do they do the things they do? I'm always looking to understand - anything, everything, everyone.

Perhaps it's because I've been misunderstood for as long as I can remember. Apart from a very few people on the planet, people really do not 'get' me. Even when I explain myself, and in great detail, the most I can usually hope for is that people accept what I've said, even if they don't quite understand.

As I was chiseling my way through 500-year-old mud (which I'm certain does get dirtier by the decade...), I couldn't help but notice how it reflected many aspects of Life. From the first moment when I realised that I would have to get rid of my pretty, old-fashioned wallpaper, which was so perfect for my English country cottage and my old style furnishings and antiques, I could see my life and my journey staring me in the face.

And therefore, I saw our common experience of dealing with change, and with life's problems, the 'animal dung' and yucky bits of life that get thrown at us. The back-breaking aches and pains of getting through stuff we don't like, don't want, stuff that hurts, day by day, or digging away inside ourselves in the pursuit of personal (and often rather painful) growth and transformation.

And I saw the many treasures that lie hidden in the dust and rubble of the miserable moments, the specific problems, and in life in general

Side by side, my dear friend and I have been chipping away at the daub in these walls. They screamed at me about how each of us is dealing with our own personal 'stuff' and life's issues, yet we're getting through it together - she and I, you and I. All of us.

I could see it again in the repointing, as my friend and I built up those 500-year-old stone walls with a better mixture to fortify, to strengthen, and to make them even more beautiful than they were with the daub stuffed in between them.

It was a lovely reminder of how change - even unwanted change - can be good for us, whether it's inside ourselves, or in our environments. It was a lovely reminder of how challenging life can be, how much it can hurt, how nasty and 'dirty' it can get but if we keep looking forward, stay focused on the progress, we get through the bumpy bits, a whole lot stronger.

It was a lovely reminder of how difficult, but how beautiful and how necessary transformation can be - transformation of yourself, a situation, your life - and how much easier it is when we share the hard parts of it with a loving friend.

The 'thinky' part of me drives many people nuts. And it can even drive me nuts, too (yes, I know, that's a very short trip...).

But I'm grateful for it because it allows me to see depth and meaning in many situations that a lot of people do not, and this adds depth and meaning to my life. In the microcosm moments of my existence, I am frequently reminded of the macrocosm years and experience of my life, and of what's really important.

I'm reminded, again and again, to embrace change, that the painful bits will pass, and to keep focused on forward movement only.

I am my stone butterfly. And you can be one, too, if you want to be.

26. "Private! Keep out! This means YOU!" Ouch.

I heard it again yesterday - a few times. Something along the lines of
"Thank you for sharing so much of yourself with us."

Most of the time, when people say this to me I'm surprised. Not that
they've said it (and it's lovely that they do), but that it's their perception that
I've done something unusual, or at least, something unusual enough that it
warrants commenting on it.

I mean, how are we supposed to get on with each other or have close and
loving relationships if we keep ourselves to ourselves?

As I keep saying on my blog, in my books and in speaking to people,
whether publicly or privately, we're all in this together - because we are.
And shouldn't we be opening ourselves up to one another and really
sharing the experience?

What experience, you ask? Well, *any*. Life, being here, the parts that hurt,
the parts that make you giggle like a little kid - and everything in between.

And if you're going to really share the experience, that includes letting
people see your pain, your fears, your celebrations and accomplishments -
and everything in between.

If you're not willing to do that, what's the point of being here? To my
mind, you're just dragging your frightened little backside through this life,
one painful, lonely minute after the next until you draw your last sad little
breath. Like a beautiful flower that never blooms, no one will ever get to
see your colours, to experience your unique and radiant spirit.

And neither will you.

When you don't let anyone else see who you really are, when you keep yourself closed off from the world, not only do you shut other people out, you shut yourself in. When you put up a barrier that says, "I'm very closed and private", you're not just saying "I don't share myself with people." You're also choosing to restrict the flow of energy, of ideas, of conversations on a level that will allow you to truly know anyone else, or to see, to understand or to access who's really on the inside of your wall.

A pond that has no source of fresh water coming in and flowing out it becomes stagnant. It becomes a swamp, so thick with algae you cannot see into its murky depths. There's nothing coming in. Nothing going out. It's unchanging and unmoving.

I would rather be a sparkling pool of crystal clear water whose shape is gradually changed by a stream rushing into it at one side and running out at the other, constantly changing and being replenished with newness and freshness.

Why do people choose to close themselves off and keep themselves private? Usually it is out of fear. Perhaps a fear that they won't be liked if people really know who they are, a fear of rejection, of being isolated.

Yet they are isolating themselves, rejecting themselves, and they will never know themselves - not fully, anyway, by not participating in their own lives as much as they could. They become what they fear.

And in doing so, they deprive themselves of really living, of experiencing all that life has to offer. Sure, they may avoid a lot of pain. But they will also miss out on a lot of joy, adventure, and the indescribable pleasure that comes from the emotional intimacy and connection of relationships with others.

Don't they see that we all have the same basic fears and desires? We want to be accepted. We want to be liked. We want companionship. We fear losing people we love. We don't want to hurt. We want to be loved.

Well, if we all share those fears and insecurities, why do we play this huge game of 'hide and seek' with each other? Why do we peek out from behind the curtains at the other kids who are playing outside and having a good time, wishing we could be out there with them, yet terrified that they'll see us at the window?

If you get brave and go outside and some of the kids don't like you, so what? Lots of others will love you.

We say that countries go to war. But it's not countries, it's people who decide to go to war, and who are dropping the bombs, using the weapons, killing each other. And when they're at war, those people do not want "the enemy" to know their next plan, their next move, their weak or vulnerable places. They want to present themselves as strong and solid. This is their only hope of survival.

But we need not live our lives as though we are at war, protecting ourselves from everyone we meet, protecting ourselves from friends, neighbours, strangers. If we do this, we are living fearful, lonely lives.

Our uniqueness is a gift from the universe. Our spirits are precious, interesting, delightful and meant to be shared with one another. It is only in that sharing that we can fully discover and express all aspects of ourselves.

When we remain closed and private, not only are we depriving others of the precious gift of knowing who we are, we are depriving ourselves, too.

It's simple. Live as though you are at war, and you will experience the pain, the isolation and the coldness that go along with it. You can be that stagnant pond, if that's what you really want.

Or you could respect that perfect gift that you've been given - the gift that is YOU - and share it with the rest of us, please, and let us enjoy it right along with you.

After all, isn't that the whole point of being here?

27. How to wave a red flag at a bully.

I suppose there are a few people on the planet who enjoy a good battle, or at least a bit of confrontation. Or perhaps it's just that they enjoy a little bullying when they can create a reason for it or when they think they're so superior that they're entitled to push the rest of us around, trample our needs and our feelings, or be disrespectful of us.

I am not one of those people.

I spent too much of my life being on the receiving end of treatment like that, and not having a clue that I had a right to stand up for myself, to stand my ground and demand to be treated with respect. That was because throughout my childhood, I learned that nothing about me mattered. I learned that I was not important but that everyone else was. I learned that I was responsible for everyone else's feelings and happiness, but that mine were not up for discussion.

I learned to keep my mouth shut or risk the consequences. And they were consequences I knew I wouldn't like. So I swallowed my feelings. I choked on my needs. I jammed an overwhelming amount of injustice down my own throat because if I didn't do it, someone else would.

This became an overriding theme in my life for decades. And it did a good deal of damage to me and to my children.

After a particularly nasty 'rock bottom' phase in my life (and there have been several), someone planted a ton of dynamite right in the middle of it and blew apart everything I'd come to believe up to that point. I will be eternally grateful to him for that because it needed to happen and it changed my life completely.

Or rather, I changed my life completely because this man showed me what needed changing and I was ready to do it.

Because of him, I learned that I did matter, that my needs and feelings were just as important as those of everyone else. I learned that I deserved to be treated with respect and that I did not - and in fact should not - have to tolerate injustice or bullying.

I learned that I had a right to speak up, to say what I think, to call others on their unfair treatment of me, whether they liked it or not.

I learned that bullies don't like it when you point out that their behaviour is out of line, no matter how appropriately you say it. They'll turn it around on you, tell you that you're just trying to pick a fight and try to make it look like you're the one who's being unreasonable.

It's because they think they're the only ones who have a right to their feelings, and who should get to say how they feel. The big difference is that they're being disrespectful of you, while you are only being assertive in appropriately and respectfully speaking your truth.

I learned to fight for what I believe is right, to fight for my principles, no matter what anyone else thinks. And I learned that sometimes, I would have to pay a high price in order to do it. But it's always been worth the cost.

I learned to choose my battles. This was one of my more difficult lessons. I expect that it will be ongoing as I continue to be presented with challenges and obstacles that are placed in front of me by people who throw their weight around, people whose insecurities manifest as arrogance, people who try to shut me up, and who are completely dismissive of my rights or my feelings.

I'm not suggesting that learning any of these lessons - and acting on them - has been easy for me.

In fact, it has been extremely difficult. To become assertive has meant healing many long-standing wounds - a process which at times was at least as painful as the initial wounding.

It has meant learning to value myself, to understand that I am just as important as everyone else and that I must treat myself accordingly.

It has meant learning *not* to keep my mouth shut, to risk the consequences, knowing that whatever they might be, they will be worth having stood up for myself. I will fight the battles that need to be fought. I will fight for my principles, for what I believe.

Because in doing so, I respect myself. I honour myself. And if I don't do that, I'll be on the receiving end of bullying for the rest of my life. This is, quite simply, not an option.

28. The sweet retreat you can have any time

I've got an enormous urge to go and sit on a curb and squish mud between my bare toes as I used to do after a prairie rain in Saskatchewan. It was so cool and soft, like liquid velvet against my sensitive skin.

As I immersed myself in this delightful little childhood memory, probably brought about by all the repointing and plaster play in my bedroom of late, my thoughts drifted like a gentle breeze from the curb in front of my house at 745 Williams Street in Regina to my mother's parents' farm near Stockholm, Sask. I was blessed to be able to spend time there every summer while I was growing up and those memories are firmly lodged deep in my heart. I suppose that to a large extent, it's because that was the only place on the planet where I ever felt safe as a child.

I remember leaping out of the cool, dark hayloft in that old red barn, the terrifying but exhilarating fall before landing in the sweet softness of a haystack below. I remember being out with my uncle and cousins collecting bales from the fields, the tractor pulling a huge flat bed with no sides, while I climbed ever higher to the top of the stack, which grew by the minute. On the bumpy journey through the fields or on the road going back to the farm, it never occurred to me that either the bales or I could fall off.

One particular summer, my cousins and I spent more time than usual in the ravine across the road, our pockets jammed with tart crabapples, hastily picked on leaving the house each morning. We found four tall, sturdy trees - couldn't tell you what kind; I was a kid and paying no attention to such things. Probably oak, as there were loads of them in the area.

We took some twine and wove little 'hammocks' for ourselves within the "Y" shaped branch formations in this little group of trees, then filled them with hay, creating nests where we spent hours on end every day. We dug a hole in the soft, damp earth right in the middle of these trees, and used an old piece of wood for a cover so we could store lemonade and a few sandwiches in our little 'cooler'.

Hour upon hour in that sweltering, slow summer, we would lie in the shade of our nests, talking, reading comics books, or adventure stories. Sometimes we even had naps, a gentle breeze stroking our hair or shoulders as a mother would do until we slept.

One night, we made a fort of bales in the farm yard, stacked two high, with a roof of plywood, and all of us piled in like sardines with sleeping bags, where we spent a dark and giggling night together.

Never once did I see the garage with its doors closed, as tools, machinery, bits of vehicles and farm equipment spilled out of them as though they'd tumbled out into the farmyard as easily as the smell of oil that went with them.

I remember being about five. It was dark one very late summer evening and my uncle was going to pick some fresh corn to add to the dinner being

prepared by my aunt. We were only across the garden, not far from the house, but it meant the world to me to be out with my Uncle Don.

Being the only one who got to go with him, I felt very special as I buried myself between the rows of corn, which was much taller than I thought I would ever be.

I will never forget the sweet smell of dough rising in my grandmother's old, blue speckled pan, which is now sitting on the hearth of my enormous inglenook fireplace. I wonder how many thousands of cinnamon buns, loaves of fresh bread and other delights came from that dough pan, made ever so lovingly by two of the softest hands and one of the kindest hearts the world has ever known.

I can still see the robin's-egg-blue painted walls in that rickety old house. I used to lie on the sagging iron bed in my room, noticing how the nails never matched up along the sides of a seam where two pieces of drywall met. That bed, that room, with the beautiful antique dresser, the washstand with pitcher and basin, that was the safest and most perfect retreat on the planet.

There was a grate on the floor next to the bed, and if I opened the slats, I could see and hear down to the dining room below. I lay in bed as a very little girl, listening to the grown-ups talking over their coffee and cake late at night, the quiet drone of their voices and the delicate clinking of cups meeting saucers lulling me to sleep.

Our fondest memories can brighten even the darkest day, and can make a good one even better. It doesn't take much to lift ourselves out of our

everyday lives and be transported to another time, another place, giving us a sweet retreat and softening the edges of the bumpiest times.

Take a few moments today... transport yourself to simpler days, happy times. Close your eyes and immerse yourself in the beautiful sights, the heartwarming sounds, the delicious smells that have imprinted themselves so lovingly in the deepest part of your heart.

Whatever kind of day you're having, this is bound to make it better.

29. The aching emptiness in my heart...

Last night, I was given a little gift that made me cry. The tears were bittersweet and spoke volumes, uttering a thousand words that my heart could not.

It was a little stuffed cat curled up asleep in a basket, with a tiny kitten sleeping on mummy's hip. As soon as I laid eyes on it, the tears bubbled up and I choked back a million sobs while clutching my kitties to my heart. I'm sure anyone watching this would have thought I'd slipped off my pulley.

For the next few hours, I could not put my kitties down. I sat here, hugging them tightly, while watching American Idol with two friends. And I was fighting waves of tears.

Am I really that nuts, you ask? Well, yes, but there are a few reasons for my weepy kitty-clutching last night, a few very painful reasons that jumped up and bit me hard the moment I saw my little gift.

I adore kitties. Always have, always will. I had cats all my life until I moved to this country several years ago, and because I was traveling back to Canada a lot to visit my family, it wouldn't have been fair on a kitty to have its mummy gone frequently and for long periods.

And it wouldn't have been fair on one kitty in particular: My sweet Petunia, whom I left behind, with one of my friends. Petunia is now 16 years old and last autumn I was there for a visit. It was the first time in all these years that she came to me on her own and climbed up onto my lap. I reckon I had finally been forgiven, although to be honest, I will probably always feel as though I don't deserve it.

She was deeply wounded when I left her. It took her 14 months to talk to me, to let me touch her or hold her even briefly when I would go back for visits. She had always been so attached to me, sleeping on my hip all night (like the kitties I got last night, with the Baby on Mummy's hip). Petunia was on my lap in a heartbeat every time I sat down, or she would climb up on the laps of my patients when they'd let her, which was most of the time.

She was devastated when I dropped her at a house she didn't know – although at least she knew the family, as they were very dear friends of mine and had spent a lot of time in my home, and she had done a fair bit of lap time with them as they were my patients, too. They've spoiled her rotten and she couldn't have been with a better family. But I've never managed to get over how much I hurt her, even though I know it was the best decision I could make for her at the time, and I'm in tears every time I think of her (like now). I miss her desperately and ache to have her on my hip again every night.

I can't have a kitty now because I have a housemate who is allergic to cats. And I'm planning a fair bit of travel in the future so I guess it's best that I don't get one now. I just wish I could have my sweet Petunia with me for her last few years of life.

Another big reason for my tearful stuffed-kitty-cuddling last night is that I'm missing my children and grandchildren so much. I did not get hugs and cuddles growing up. Quite the opposite, in fact. It was a very cold and abusive environment.

Starved for love and being affectionate by nature, since I began having my own children (I was a teenager at the time), I have been a very cuddly mummy, which soon spread to being a cuddly friend, too. And a cuddly "Grams" when my grandchildren came along.

But my whole family is in Calgary. Five children, five (for now) grandchildren. I got stuck on the other side of the planet, unable to visit as often now as had been the case when I moved here.

I ache to see them, to hold them, to play with them, to "love 'em up" and the very powerfully maternal part of me has a huge, gaping hole in it. I've got all this Mama love to give and the phone and internet only go so far in allowing me to do that. Or perhaps it's the little girl who is looking to connect in that way. I reckon the reason is irrelevant anyway.

There are many special people in Canada whom I miss, people my arms want to hug, my heart needs to hug…but I am here and they are there. So I do the next best thing.

I hug other people wherever and whenever I can. I'm the 'Mama ear' for many people. I cuddle kitties in the village who wander into my garden, and I feed one of them whose parents can't be bothered and the poor little thing is terribly skinny and always in my rubbish bins.

If I can't be doing my Mama and Grams cuddle thing in person across the pond, I will do it here in England for those who need it. And if I can't cuddle my sweet Petunia or another kitty that could be my own, I will cuddle and feed the starving kitty in my garden.

I can still do my best to offer love and affection via phone or internet to loads of people who can use a supportive or encouraging word. I never tire of it because I know how it feels to need it as much as air or food.

But my arms still ache for my babies, my grandbabies, and my kitty. So last night, I cuddled my new stuffed kitty and the baby on her hip (as my Petunia used to be on mine).

And I cried.

30. Letting Go and Welcoming In...

A miracle has been developing in recent weeks. Through a series of smaller miracles, one after another, last night it was right here, announcing itself in a bigger way. I'm so happy this morning, I don't know what to do with myself!

Years ago, in about the mid-'90s, I read an article about how women really need the support and friendship for all aspects of their health and wellbeing. Studies proved that women who have a strong group of friends with whom they can talk and spend time together are healthier and recover quicker from illness than women who feel isolated and alone.

I remember thinking about how lucky I was because I did have such a group of friends. I lived in Calgary at the time and had a large group of close friends so there were lots of occasions for me to go out for lunch with someone, or have someone in for a pizza and a bottle of wine. And I had one very close friend who lived in Toronto but she came to see me twice a year for about ten days, with twice-weekly phone calls in between to keep us very connected in between those delicious visits.

Then I moved to England several years ago. I'm very blessed to have maintained many of those friendships - and in fact, some of them have even got closer with phone and internet. But for some reason, I've really struggled to find people right in my area with whom I could get together for frequent in-person visits. There have been a few, but visits have been sporadic and there's been a massively enormous hole in my life where friends and socialising used to be. I felt desperately alone and lonely for the first several years after moving here, aching for lots of time spent in the company of women friends.

I can't tell you how lost and empty I felt because of that big hole. And because of my already very poor physical health, on top of a lot of emotional turmoil, I worried about how my lack of an in-person group of close friends was affecting me long-term.

A couple of years ago, I began to look at it from the Buddhist perspective - that all suffering comes from attachment, and if I could stop being attached to my need for such a group, if I could let go of my desire to spend time with women friends, I would stop hurting.

It wasn't easy and it didn't happen overnight, but over the next year or two, gradually I accepted that this was how my life was meant to be and I stopped agonising about it. I let go of the wishing and the frustration, and accepted my situation.

Recently, I was finally able to organise having gatherings of people in my home to discuss a variety of topics of an emotional and/or spiritual nature. Anything to do with overcoming obstacles, or helping us deal with the stuff life lobs at us, or progressing on our journeys.

I wanted these gatherings to have a starting point - a topic for the night - but I didn't want structure, didn't want them to be about me blah blah blahing at a room full of listeners. I wanted them to be a mutual sharing and exchange of ideas, information and energy, so we could all learn from each other, and wherever the conversation flowed would be exactly where it needed to go, even if we ended up way off the original topic.

Although I figured that there would be mostly women attending, men would be welcome, too, because male and female perspectives are often quite different and therefore, we can learn a lot from the opposite sex.

Last night was the first meeting. The topic was "letting go" and there was a lovely group of women here (whom I met when they came to other recent mini-events I had at my home). There are others who plan to attend, at least sometimes, both men and women, and I'm very excited to see how this develops. I think there will be a core group who are usually here, with others coming and going, depending on what the scheduled topics are.

This would be perfect! Some continuity with a regular group, with new energy flowing in and out, changing week to week, offering fresh perspectives, different opinions, someone else's life experience and insights - this is what I envision.

Last night, near the end of the conversation, I commented on this issue I had for years after moving here, not having a group of like-minded women with whom I could be close and spend lots of time, and now all of a sudden, I've found several of them right on my doorstep, living nearby and looking for the same thing.

I added that I couldn't help but notice that it was only after I was able to let go of my attachment to the need, let go of the aching about it, that I'd finally found it. I've met some lovely women through these recent meetings in my home, most of whom came to me through recent village hall events I did, which led to Facebook connections - and now that I've established this weekly gathering, I'm absolutely thrilled.

With my heart filled to overflowing last night with appreciation for the women who were in attendance, and for the other people I've met recently and who are planning to come in the future, I smiled as I realised what a perfect topic I'd chosen for this first and very special gathering. For so long, I'd felt such pain in not having a group of friends nearby. Letting go of that need turned out to be the way to relieve the pain.

And as soon as I was able to do it and be at peace with it, I was given exactly what my heart desired all those previous years in this country.

I am truly blessed by having met such a lovely group of people in recent weeks and I welcome them (and others I've not yet met) into my home and my heart.

I'm looking forward to getting to know them, to developing new friendships, and seeing where our journeys take us together.

31. Living in your Authentic Power

Your perception of power, and what makes anyone powerful, no matter who it is, is all in your mind. It is what you believe it to be.

If you attach your sense of power and control to sources outside yourself (eg. job, status, relationship, money, car etc), you become vulnerable and fearful because these can be lost. In a state such as that, you might then try to take power and control from others.

In general, we tend to place too much emphasis on power that comes from external sources. The more of it people have, the more value we place on those people. But if you take away whatever it is that we see as giving them power (money, status, job etc.), they become just like everyone else – vulnerable and fearful.

I remember Edith Bunker on "All In The Family" saying, "I can imagine the Queen brushing her teeth, but I can't imagine her spittin' it out!" Well, the truth is, if you take away the title of "Queen" and everything associated with it, she's just a regular person like the rest of us.

The lawyer gets turfed from the Bar. The doctor loses his license. The priest leaves the church. The perfect face is scarred in a fire. The athlete ends up in a wheelchair. The wife is abandoned by her husband.

If these people had their identities and sense of power tied up in their jobs, their accomplishments, their relationships, they would perceive these changes as catastrophic.

But if they have authentic power, they won't feel as though they've lost control of their lives. They won't be feeling vulnerable, fearful, or powerless.

Feeling powerless is not the same as being powerless. In reality, most of the time when you think you're powerless in a situation, you really aren't. But this feeling prevents you from seeing the truth. It prevents you from seeing your options. And usually, it comes from something outside of yourself.

If you have a weak leg and rely on crutches, you will fear someone knocking your crutches out from under you, or you might fear dropping them, because this would make you vulnerable. The crutches make you think you're okay but take one or both away and you become fearful, weak and vulnerable.

Authentic power is generated from inside you and it is the only kind of power that is lasting, and that gives you complete control. No one can knock you off balance; no one can take it from you so you never have to feel fearful or vulnerable.

When you're operating out of your own authentic power, it drives every choice you make. You will never need or want to control others, or situations.

What is authentic power? It is the energy produced and felt when focused intention is based in love and guided by the wisdom of your Higher Self. When you are following that wisdom, your life and choices will reflect this. You will feel strong, confident, in control of your life.

Living in your authentic power means speaking your truth, and walking in it, too. It means accepting all parts of yourself and loving them unconditionally. It means accessing your Higher Self, the wisdom of your soul, and letting it guide you in all your thoughts, words and deeds.

This is the greatest power there is and it offers the greatest possible freedom and ability to be all you're meant to be.

32. Your thoughts are valuable currency. Spend wisely.

What were you thinking about just before you began reading this? Or in the previous hour? What is the subject of your thoughts a lot of the time?

While you're going about your business, at work, doing your chores, while driving, gardening, or in the shower, what's on your mind?

Are you thinking about your plans for the future? Your goals? Or are you thinking about what's wrong in your life or what's missing?

Are you busy being resentful? Dwelling on long-ago issues and events that can never be changed, and only perpetuate the misery that you lived back then?

When you're thinking about what's wrong, or how much your life sucks right now, you're not thinking about how to put it right and make it better. You become part of the problem and reduce the possibility of finding a solution – or at least, you will significantly delay it.

The more time you spend dwelling on your current state of discontent, the less time you have to do anything about it. Your future will become more of what you're living and thinking about right now.

What you're *not* thinking about is just as important as what you *are* thinking about.

Let's say you want to buy one beautiful ring set with flawless, perfect diamonds, but you cannot afford it. You really, really want it but all you can afford is the cheap imitation stuff. You know that if you want that diamond ring badly enough, you'll have to be disciplined, spending your money wisely so you can have it someday.

But you don't like the sacrifices. You have to give up the meals out, the fast food, the cinema. You have to start making a conscious choice to change your habits. You tell yourself you'll make do with the cheap costume jewellery for now, and someday when you have more money, you'll buy that beautiful sparkling diamond ring.

You are always in control of the thoughts in your head. If you don't like them, change them. If the miserable ones keep coming, keep replacing them with positive, helpful ones. Don't beat yourself up about it (a further waste of thoughts, time and energy) – just stick a new, happy thought in there and move on.

"But it's hard!" you say. Maybe. And so what if it is? Does that mean it's not worth it? And even if it is difficult to start, it does get easier with practice.

If you're frivolous with how you spend your thoughts, if you waste them on the "junk jewellery" of life, you'll be just as dissatisfied as ever, and you'll never have that sparkling radiant diamond that's just waiting to be yours.

33. A fairy tale of battery acid and cream

Once upon a time, there was a girl called Glumella who lived in a tiny house in the woods. She was a miserable little thing who sipped on battery acid and ate the prickliest thistles she could find.

Gradually, she became increasingly sour, shrivelling up just a teeny bit more every day.

She was always waiting for things to get worse and was comforted when they did, relieved not to have wasted any energy on being hopeful, only to end up disappointed.

"I knew it!" she'd mutter to herself, because no one dared come within 100 miles of her miserableness. No one, that is, but her very beautiful little sister, Miss Perky-Lee.

Glumella was very jealous of Perky-Lee, whose entire being radiated sparkly sunshine and everything lovely. This sweet girl just couldn't wait to get up every morning. She was always so excited about another new day, she just had to sprinkle her sunniness on anyone and everyone she met.

She lived on fresh cream and berries and never had a harsh word for anyone. Not even her miserable older sister, whom she adored and whose nastiness went unnoticed by the younger of the two.

In days gone by, Glumella used to wish she could be like her little sister, who was eternally happy, had loads of friends and was always dashing off to do something fun.

"Come on, Glumella!" the bubbly girl would coax. "We'll have such a good time!"

But the grouchy older sister refused, for no particular reason, preferring instead to stay home alone, sipping on battery acid and eating the prickliest of thistles.

Eventually, Perky-Lee would stop pleading and head for the door and her waiting friends. "You know where I am if you change your mind!" she said every time. "I hope you join us later, my beloved sister!"

Her lips already just a thin, tight line, Glumella pursed them even more with every cheery little note that came out of her sister's mouth. Her eyes were even squintier and I swear she shrivelled up a wee bit more with every syrupy syllable that assaulted her tiny, dried-up ears.

One day, Glumella could take no more. She could not stand to hear one more excited, delighted word from her cheery little sister. As soon as Perky-Lee leapt out of bed, Glumella was ready and waiting to grab her and stuff her into a dark and empty closet. Slamming the door shut and locking it, the older sister smiled in smug self-satisfaction.

"I'll teach her a lesson!" she snarled. "I'll show her that life is miserable and empty and horrible and there's absolutely nothing in it that should make her so nauseatingly happy all the time!"

She waited for the screams, the pleading and the pounding, but they never came. Instead, Perky-Lee maintained her composure.

"Please, dear Sister, would you open the door? I seem to have got stuck in this closet," she said quietly.

Glumella was puzzled.

"Silly me, I don't know how it happened!" Perky-Lee continued. "But here I am, dear Sister, and the door is jammed. Could you help me, please?"

Glumella's eyebrows knit themselves together. Still, she did not utter a sound. Instead, she shoved a saucer of battery acid and a plate of thistles under the door for her sister to eat, and ran from the house.

It was dark when she returned that evening, making her way through the woods to her little home. But as she grew closer, she could see a soft light glowing in the windows.

"What's this?" she wondered. She hadn't left any lights on. Perhaps Perky-Lee's friends had come in and – oh, dear, those meddlesome little brats had better not have let her out of that closet!

Quickening her pace, she hurried to the house and went inside. There were no friends. The closet door was still locked. No lamps were lit. But there was a soft light radiating from the closet and filling the little house. And she heard only a lovely, quiet tune as Perky-Lee sang softly to herself on the other side of that locked door.

As Glumella stared at the door and the light, she saw the saucer and plate being shoved back. But she was stunned to see that the saucer was filled with cream and the plate was filled with berries.

"How did you — where —" Glumella could not finish the questions. Terrified, she ran from the house once again.

By the light of day, she thought she was brave enough to return once more. But the light was growing even brighter than before and there were more saucers of cream and plates of berries. And still that infernal singing!

For days, Glumella kept shoving battery acid and thistles under the door for her sister then disappearing into the woods. And every time she returned, the light shone brighter, and the plates were filled with berries and cream.

One night, as she stood dumbfounded again and staring at those plates, she noticed that the light was warm. Perhaps it had been warm before; she did not know. All that mattered was that it was warm just then, and that was unfamiliar. She thought, perhaps, that it was even pleasant, and did not realise that until that very moment, she had always been cold.

She stood unmoving and in awe as the warmth from her sister's light wrapped her in a loving embrace, while one tear chased another down her dry and withered cheek. Hesitantly, she bent down and plucked a berry from the plate, and popped it in her mouth. Its sweetness was foreign and beautiful at the same time; Glumella could not wait for another. And another. And still another.

Suddenly, there was a loud click as the door unlocked itself and the radiant Miss Perky-Lee stepped out of the closet. Glumella burst into sobs as she fell into her little sister's arms, begging to be forgiven.

But Miss Perky-Lee simply smiled and held her sister, knowing that there was nothing to forgive.

34. Destination unknown. But I don't care.

I'm a very determined woman. You could call me strong-willed; that'd work, too. Some would just say stubborn. But didja ever notice that people call it 'strong-willed' when they approve of what you're doing, and 'stubborn' when they don't?

Whatever it is, I've got it.

Interestingly, I've also got the ability to change and adapt very easily. Supposedly a Pisces trait, being a water sign, but whether it's because of personality or astrology, thank heaven I've got both ends of the spectrum covered so I can dig in my heels when I need to do it, and I can bend when that's the best option.

The trick has been to learn when to be 'strong-willed' and not 'stubborn', and when to be adaptable and not a doormat, changing just to please everyone else.

I've had to learn to choose my battles carefully and believe me, I've done that the very hard way - which is pretty much the same way I've learned everything else, to be honest. Part of the problem is that I'm a woman of principle. If I believe in something, if I think something is unfair, if I hear my dad in my head saying "It's the principle of the thing!" as he used to do, it's really difficult for me to back down.

I suppose this is what helps me when I'm confronted with huge obstacles. When things just aren't working out as planned, I just have to keep knocking on doors. If this one doesn't open, maybe that one will. And if not that one, then perhaps another one.

Sometimes I've knocked on so many unanswered doors, I've felt like I was in a condemned building where no one has lived for years.

So then what?

I keep knocking. Perhaps the building isn't condemned. Perhaps there will be an answer at just one of those doors, and that's all I need. And if I run out of doors in that building, I move on to the next one and start knocking there. I mean, what else am I gonna do? Sit there on the street and do nothing? That sure as heck won't open any doors for me.

So I might as well keep knocking. At least that way, there's a chance of getting an answer. Giving up is not an option. Not ever. Switch hands when your knuckles get sore. Grab an object to do the knocking for you when both sets of knuckles are bleeding and raw. But keep knocking.

Is that being strong-willed? Stubborn? Determined? I don't know. Perhaps. Or maybe it's just understanding that if we really want to change our situations, we have to do something. It doesn't work if you just sit there and wish.

Sometimes busting your backside doesn't work either. But then at least you can say you gave it your best shot and you won't spend the rest of your life wondering, "what would have happened if..."

If it's worth wanting, it's worth the effort. If you're not willing to put in the effort, then stop wanting it.

Whether it's complaining about your job or your relationship or your lack of physical fitness or your bad habits or your garden that's way too full of weeds or that book you said you'd write or 14,000,000 other things that you keep talking about fixing or changing, do it. Keep knocking on doors till you get the answer that works, till you find the solution, till the opportunity is the right one.

It's a lot easier to do that, than it is to stop wanting what you really want.

35. Don't expect your life to bring you joy. Bring joy to your life.

Life should not be about finding the way to happiness. Instead, happiness should be the way of life - the way *to* Life.

There's a good chance you're thinking, yeah, sure, with all the misery in life, how is that possible? How can you be happy when things are in turmoil, when difficult or terrible things are happening to you or to the people you love?

Well, that's the challenge. I didn't say it was easy. But it's well worth pursuing.

I've lived through some pretty awful stuff. That doesn't make me special; I know very well that I'm not alone (which is the point of having books, meditation CDs and a blog that are all about inspirational and healing work). I've met very few people who have said they've had relatively happy and uncomplicated lives. Most of us have a story, one that is filled with pain and disappointment.

I'm only mentioning my very difficult life because I want you to understand that I'm not just talking the talk, I'm walking the walk. I know what it is to suffer, to have terrible experiences, to be at the bottom of a big, dark hole and to fight my way out of it.

My reason for telling you that is to say I'm living proof that it's possible to do it. You just have to decide it's what you want.

One of the best places to begin is to accept that all conditions of life serve a higher purpose. Now, I realise that you may not agree with that because people don't all share the same beliefs. But the way I see it, I'd rather believe that there is some good, some purpose, some reason for the rotten things that happen to us, than believe it's just a random bunch of miserableness. My belief about there being a purpose to all of it has helped me get through an awful lot. And I do mean "awful".

If you can accept the difficulties and the horrible parts of your life as serving a higher purpose, this removes the angst, the struggle, and gives you peace. I can't even begin to tell you how wonderful it feels to do that, to let go of the frustration, the worry, the anger, the regret. It is the sweetest relief when you can simply sink into a state of acceptance - like when you've endured horrific physical pain for a long period, or you've been extremely ill, and then the pain stops, the illness goes and there is nothing where they used to be, nothing but peace.

The next step is in understanding that the search for happiness leads to anxiety, worry, competition and disappointment because once we have the desired object or situation that we believed would bring us happiness, the happiness fades and more desires for other objects or situations take its place. That kind of happiness is superficial and short-lived. And there's never a guarantee that you'll even get it. Searching does not guarantee success.

When we expect external events or other people to bring joy to our lives, more often than not this will only bring disappointment. It makes more sense to bring joy to every event, every day, every moment, every person. It is the only kind of joy that lasts because it is completely within your control, as it comes from inside you - from a choice that you've made to bring that perspective to your life as you're living it.

Do not expect your life to bring you joy. Instead, bring joy to your life. This is the only way to lasting and true happiness.

36. Travel light. And I don't mean luggage.

Travel light. Let go of pain. Forgive. Let go of the past. It does not exist, except in your thoughts. It can only hurt you if you let it. Look ahead - and only ahead, for that is the only place you can still have some influence.

Begin each day with a clean slate. Wash away the anger, guilt, regret, hurt, worry from days before. They've had their chance, they've taken their toll. Do not forget the lessons you learned from those troubles but let that be all you carry forward from those experiences.

Allow yourself the freedom and release that come from leaving your pain behind you. Allow yourself to replace all dwelling and miserable thoughts with what you desire, how you plan to be, how you are healed and healing, changed and changing, how much stronger and wiser you are and will be.

One sad truth about life is that there are few things you can control. But one of these is among the most important. You can control your thoughts.

Yes. You really can. But only if you're willing to make the effort.

Imagine you're on your deathbed. You're reflecting on your life. The sand has almost run out of your hourglass. Are you going to remember fondly all the time you spent dwelling, regretting, agonising, and worrying? Are you going to consider any of that as having been time well spent?

When you're running out of minutes - and that day really will come - you will wish you'd spent all the previous minutes as wisely and lovingly as possible. You will wish you had not wasted a single precious moment on harbouring any negativity, whether it was directed at yourself or someone else. You'll see how it tainted your life with toxic black sludge and you will wish you had let every bit of it go.

So do it now and save yourself that grief at the end of your life.

Forgive yourself.

You must be at peace with yourself to have authentic power, and to be truly happy. If there are parts of yourself that trouble you, change what you can, apologise where you should, forgive others, forgive yourself and *let it all go.*

There is more healing in offering an apology than in countless hours in a therapist's office. If you know you owe an apology to someone, give it. Even if the person has moved, disappeared, died - do it on paper, in your mind or in your heart. Offer it anyway. The Universe will deliver your healing message. It's a huge step toward your finding peace.

Be sure to apologise to yourself for beating yourself up, for negative self-talk, self-destructive behaviour, regrets and guilt.

And then, remember that an apology means you're honestly not intending to do the offending 'thing' again - so don't go sliding back into regret and hurting yourself with nasty thoughts again.

Strive for purity of heart and mind by emptying them of negative, destructive and hurtful thoughts, whether directed at yourself or anyone else. This will keep you connected to your Higher Self, which will help you to make the best choices on your path to a happy and fulfilled life.

And remember: every moment is a chance to begin again.

37. "I can't" vs. "I haven't done it - yet."

Throughout my life, from being a little kid right up until my mother got dementia and she was no longer herself, she told me what I couldn't do. Okay, there's some stuff mums are supposed to tell you that you can't do.

Like throw yourself off the roof of your three-storey house when you're playing Superman because really, honestly, no doubt about it, you will not be able to fly. No, not even with your beach-towel cape clothes-pinned to the shoulders of your T-shirt.

No, I'm not talking about the kind of "You can't" that means you're not allowed for reasons of safety, health etc. I'm talking about the kind that says you won't be able to do it so don't even bother trying.

I wanted to try this or that new thing and was always told, "You can't." I was told I'd get it wrong or mess it up or simply be unable because I was too stupid.

And of course, if I did try and she turned out to be right, I got the ITYS three-course special crammed down my throat, right from "I told you so" for the starter, through to the smug look smothered in superiority for the main course, followed by the rather tart dessert, "You think you know so much."

The older I got, the more I dared try things that I "wouldn't be able to do because I wasn't 'something' enough." Looking back, her words make me smile now because they're just so ridiculous. How could she know I "couldn't" when I hadn't even tried?

But as a kid (and even later as an adult), that never occurred to me. I just believed her because she was my mother.

I was just listening to Fantasie Impromptu Opus 66 in C sharp minor – one of my favourite pieces of music, and one of Chopin's best known works and, in my opinion, one of the most beautiful pieces ever written. It's insanely fast and complicated – until you get to the middle bit which slows and becomes deliciously romantic with one note melting into the next like rich chocolate blends into thick cream.

I was thinking about how I've learned that beautiful middle bit with no problem, but am wistfully waiting for the day when I can get the insanely fast parts down, too. Although I can play the millions of notes that run up and down the keyboard, I'm nowhere near fast enough.

It feels a bit daunting when I listen to it. But then I remember a summer when I was 19. My mother came upon an ancient piece of sheet music that was her father's. "Meditation" from the opera, Thais. She said, "Oh, this is beautiful! This was his favourite piece of music. But you could never play it. It's way too hard."

I suppose she'd forgotten about some of the extremely complicated and lengthy pieces that my music teacher had me playing on television, radio, at the Calgary Stampede and at various other venues and in competitions when I was as young as 12 or 13.

A few weeks later, on a rainy Monday, with no one else around, I spent eight hours at the piano. By Tuesday at noon, I had this piece memorised. It wasn't nearly as difficult as the ones my teacher had given me years earlier.

In fact, I thought it was relatively simple. But it certainly one of the most beautiful I've ever heard.

It was one of very many lessons in my life about the difference between "I can't" and "I haven't done it yet."

What's kind of funny is that the next time I saw my mother, I couldn't wait for her to hear that I'd learned this song. I was so excited and thought that – for once – she might actually be proud of me, be pleased with something I'd done.

Without a word, I sat down at the piano while she puttered in the house and I began to play.

I got every note right. I played with lots of feeling (there is no other way to play anything, as far as I'm concerned). When I was finished, I waited for her to be surprised, to be impressed, to be amazed that I'd learned it flawlessly and so quickly.

But she made no comment. She continued puttering with her chores, as if she had not heard me play at all. I asked if she recognised the piece, hoping to get some sort of positive reaction. "No," came her disinterested reply.

I told her what it was. She said it wasn't at all familiar and that perhaps there's some other piece called "Meditation" that my grandfather loved (which, as it turned out, was the case, and that piece was extremely simple by comparison and I couldn't believe she had thought *that* one would have been too complicated for me!).

At the time, this was all rather upsetting but I can laugh at myself now, and I see how far I've come because eventually, with many lessons and a lot of healing, I stopped seeking my mother's (or anyone else's) approval.

I'm still carefully picking my way through the speedy part of Chopin's Fantasie Impromptu as though I'm walking barefoot through thistles. And sometimes I get impatient because I'm not playing it quickly and the only part I do as it should be done is the slower middle bit. Occasionally, my mother wanders through my head and tells me I can't do it, but I just smile and whisper to her in the spirit world. "Yes, I can, Mum. I just haven't done it…yet."

38. Just a spoonful of sugar... or "Healer, heal thyself!"

I need a dose of medicine. And a fairly good-sized one, at that. In fact, I could use a bottle or two. And the medicine is my own.

I've gotta stop working 18 or 19 hours a day. I do this at weekends, too. I'm not good at 'time off' because I love what I do and it doesn't feel like work. I'm having a good time so I just keep going and going and going...rather like the Energizer Bunny.

I may not have noticed all that work, but my body certainly has. And it's rebelling. It knows that I got really busy with "work", then turned around one day to discover that I've stopped doing yoga. I've stopped studying Italian. I've stopped eating proper meals (or even proper grazing 'meals' and am living on a bite of this and a little snack on that).

I've not slept well for 36 years (what an understatement) so I used to have naps on my worst days but oops, I've stopped doing that, too. I can be absolutely wrung out and desperate for sleep, but I keep going, saying I'll nap later, later, later. And it never happens.

And I've stopped doing my "practice writing" which I loved so much. It's completely different from my regular writing (books, blog etc. on the computer). "Practice writing" is a daily exercise that involves a fountain pen and a notebook, writing on a specific topic without stopping at all, just a completely free-flowing bunch of words, there's no going back to correct, no stopping to think about it, just writing writing writing for a set time, or number of pages.

And when I did my practice writing, sometimes I came up with some wonderful insights and ideas because it was like meditating when I got into 'that zone' and everything just flowed and there was no stopping, no restriction. It felt absolutely wonderful and was very freeing.

For me, writing is a not just a hobby, a passion, it is like food and air. And it's the same with wanting to reach out and help people. I want to do it. I love to do it. So I'm happy to be here at the other end of an email or a Facebook message to offer my support and some encouragement.

But because "work" for me is so enjoyable and is just a natural extension of who I am, I didn't notice that my life is now very lopsided and out of balance.

My body has noticed, though. It's been trying to tell me this but I've not been paying attention. For several months, I've had extreme pain in my right arm, shoulder and hand - a repetitive strain injury from too much computer time.

It took me ages to figure out why it was hurting so much, and just kept getting worse to the point where I've had a lot of pain just getting dressed, turning on a light, brushing my teeth or combing my hair.

I could ignore those quite easily as I've lived with chronic pain for over 30 years. But recently, I've had other reminders that are much more 'in my face' and are demanding to be noticed.

So - oops. Okay. The Big Universal slap upside the head has been duly noted. Got it.

Note to self: Take your own medicine, liberty. Remember about balance. Go for a walk. Do some yoga. Do your practice writing. Finish writing the music for those two albums you started. Haul out the Italian lessons again. Eat! Don't just graze while you continue to work!

And for heaven's sake, would you take a nap???

Yeah, yeah, yeah. I get it!

Man, I can be such a nag!

39. Chiropractics for the soul

Everything you think and do, everything about your life, your experiences, contributes to the development of your soul. The people with whom you associate, the way you spend your spare time, the jobs you hold, your relationships to other people, your emotional experiences, whether positive or negative - everything you do, everything you experience will become a part of you, your history, your learning.

Every choice you make in every moment of your life is duly noted by your soul - your spirit. It wants you to make the right choices, the ones which are in alignment with your Highest Self, to living an authentic life, the ones which bring you closer to a connection with the Divine, and which will allow you to be a beacon, lighting the way for others, whether they are seekers of spiritual enlightenment, or lost and troubled souls.

All of those difficult human lessons of struggle, suffering and sacrifice, and your reactions to them, must be used for your betterment. When you experience love, hate, selfishness, jealousy, joy, greed, anger, happiness, every bit of it is observed by your soul and either helps or hinders your spiritual development.

As you make your way down that path, be conscious of the thoughts you think, the choices you make, for every single one of them is being observed by your soul. It wants the best for you and is speaking silently to you, whispering in the quietest part of your heart, its words of wisdom helping and urging you move forward and keeping your choices in alignment with your Highest Self.

40. On living an empowered life

Your authentic power is yours, and only yours. No one else can touch it.
No one else can diminish it, change it, add to it or take away from it. You
are the only one who is in control of it. Now isn't that a most empowering
thought?

To create authentic power – and then maintain it – you must ignore all
intentions except the ones that will create harmony, strength and fulfillment
in yourself and in your life. One thought at a time, one moment at a time,
one choice at a time, your intentions will manifest as your authentic power.

Understanding how to create authentic power is easier than actually doing
it. But it's the same for anything else that allows you to grow and develop.

Besides, there's nothing wrong with it being a bit of a challenge – or even a
lot of a challenge – because it's well worth the effort, and once you're living
in your authentic power, it is its own reward.

All you really need in order to achieve this is the desire for it. Then, one
thought, one moment, one choice at a time, you keep practicing until it
becomes easier. If you don't know how to play the piano, you can't sit
down today and play a Fugue by Bach. But you can start taking lessons and
if you really want to play that Fugue, if you practice enough, someday you'll
get there.

Keep your eye on where you want to be. If you focus on your desires, your
concentration becomes determination, which fuels your intentions. Then
watch for them to manifest as your authentic power and enjoy a
harmonious, fulfilled life.

41. Challenge yourself. You're worth it.

Do you want to progress in your life? Do you want to grow and develop personally and spiritually?

Although it's absolutely none of my business, I hope you said "Yes" to those questions because personally, I think life would be pretty dull otherwise (but that's just my opinion, of course).

If you did answer "Yes", prepare for challenge. Prepare to be faced with people who push your buttons. They'll be presenting you with opportunities to choose how you react. Will it be with anger, jealousy or fear? Or will it be with love, tolerance, acceptance, or a look inside yourself to see what needs healing? Will you choose action or reaction? Will you act on your desire for learning and growth, opportunities to stretch yourself in search of a harmonious life?

When you're challenged in this way, you must remember to think about your intentions. What are they, and what do you hope to accomplish? If you don't know the answer to those questions, you won't be able to grow or deepen your sense of self-awareness.

You have to know where you're starting if you want to get to the end. You can't get there if you've been blindfolded and spun around a bunch of times so you don't even know what direction to take.

To create authentic power, you have to be completely aware of yourself, your feelings and your intentions. If you're in a state of unawareness, you can't possibly fix or change them in a way that is going to be purposeful and help you along your path. As Dr Phil McGraw says, "You can't fix what you don't acknowledge."

First, you have to know what needs changing – or what you want to change. This will tell you what your intentions are and this will help you make choices that are in alignment with them.

There is often a battle between the soul, and human desires, emotions and ego. So you will be challenged by your intentions, whatever they are. You will be challenged by your fear, betrayal, anger, any painful emotions that you are allowing to control you.

When you stop allowing it, you take back the control and you are behind the wheel, just where you should be.

It takes time and practice but with the right intentions, you will create authentic power if that's what you want. If it is your intention, the choice has already been made.

42. Books, covers, judgement and treasure boxes.

Come on, let's be honest. We've all got some insecurities. Some of us have more than others. Some of us work at healing them so they don't bite us in the backside too badly. But we've all got 'em, whether we want to admit it or not. They're part of the human condition.

It's also very normal for us to want to be accepted, to want approval, to want to fit in, to belong to a group. It's innate; we need that need for our survival. Even the most spiritually evolved people need it.

Taken to the extreme, in order to make my point, they might say they do not in any way, shape or form require the acceptance of another. But they would struggle if there were absolutely no people at all in their lives, if they had to live a life of complete isolation, or if there was not one other person on the planet who liked them, accepted them, would speak to them.

Those people might be able to lift themselves out of their fearful, anxious or insecure moments a lot quicker than some other people, but they've all got them - because they are human, which means they can never be perfect.

Part of being an imperfect human means that we can tend to judge. Sometimes we do it without even noticing, and this is because to some extent, we have to judge in order to survive. Is this situation safe? Will this person cause me harm?

So there is a natural judging that goes on in ours heads without us even noticing. I like this person. I hate that colour. I don't like her dress. He is so irritating. That's a stupid TV show. This movie sucks. That person is boring. This book is exciting. I would never do that! What a flake! I love how he plays the piano. And on and on and on.

Sometimes Life throws situations and events at us that are really awful, or that cause us embarrassment. Sometimes we do it to ourselves because of the choices we've made - and we didn't think them through or they didn't go as planned, but the bottom line is, we end up in some kind of mess that we think makes us look bad.

In part, it's because we know we can make judgements about others - even when we try not to do it - and we know, or expect, or fear that others are making judgements about us.

We've done things that are 'outside the box', unconventional, that go against the grain, that will raise eyebrows, that will shock, that will offend, that will make us look like fools - the list goes on and on.

And boy, do I ever know that stuff well... There's so much about my life that just begs people to judge me in a very negative way, to think I'm a complete flake. They can look at situations in which I found myself, or events that have happened to me.

They can look at what I've done in my life. They can look at how many times I've been married, how many times I've moved, changed jobs, changed religions, changed names, and immediately think I'm a scatterbrain, I'm flighty, I'm just a big mess.

But they *don't* know far more than they *do* know about me. And if they want to judge, I don't give a rat's @$$. Besides, just because most people do things a certain way, why does that have to be the only way, the 'right' way? Why does it automatically mean that another way is wrong, bad, faulty, flawed, or just plain nuts?

On paper, I look really unstable. I look like someone you wouldn't want to touch with a ten-foot-pole. In reality, there is an awful lot more to the picture. I am an extremely complicated woman, not that I try to be, but I just am.

Some people are uncomplicated. What you see is what you get. Like a good book with a clear and unambiguous title. Open it up and the pages give you just exactly what you expected.

But sometimes, that book isn't really a book. Sometimes, you take it off the shelf, lift the cover and discover that it's one of those pretend books that's really a secret hiding place for all kinds of treasures or trinkets, a collection of weird stuff, little odds and ends, and you had no idea what would be inside.

What's happened or happening on the outside, the situations in which you have found yourself do not define who you are. Only you can do that by the thoughts you think, the beliefs you hold, the intentions you have and what's important to you. All of those are of your own choosing.

Never mind what has happened to you, what situations life has thrown at you. Whether you chose them or not is irrelevant. What anyone else thinks about them - or about you because of them - is irrelevant because those situations are not YOU.

43. If you keep doing what you're doing, you'll keep getting what you've got.

Imagine this: Every morning, you get up, go to the kitchen and put on a pot of coffee. While that's brewing, you haul out a frying pan, put it on some heat and chuck in some butter.

Next, you get a little bowl. You throw in an egg, a bit of milk and a pinch of salt. You mix it all up, drop a piece of bread in the bowl, flip it over to coat both sides, and once that butter is melted, you place it in the pan.

It's golden on the bottom after a few minutes, so you flip it over. When the second side is also cooked, it goes on a plate and you cover it with jam and a light dusting of icing sugar (or perhaps you'd prefer syrup on yours).

You get your cup of coffee and you eat your French toast for breakfast. Every day. Same thing.

But you'd really love bacon and a fried egg. Or a bowl of soup. Or fresh muffins.

Somehow, none of those ever appears while you're melting the butter in the pan and mixing the egg and milk every morning. It always turns out to be French toast and coffee.

Are you dissatisfied with your job? Do you keep saying the same things over and over again in an effort to resolve problems with your partner, your parent, your child? Do you feel discontented, restless, stuck and frustrated, knowing something needs to change but then not changing it?

Well, as long as you don't change it, it won't change. Unless, of course, someone else does the changing first but if you're going to wait for that, you might be waiting till they're selling ice cream in The Very Hot Place.

If your words aren't being heard and the problems are not being resolved, find different words, a different approach, another tactic. If you hate your job, start looking for a new one or turn a hobby into a business on the side and build it up over time. If you're tired of doing the same old things, then find some more exciting new ones.

The bottom line is, if your life needs to change, then change it. The possibilities for ways to improve it, to get it moving, to make it better, are endless.

But one thing's for sure. If you keep doing what you're doing, you'll keep getting what you've got.

44. Oh dear! What will the neighbours think??!

Do you worry about what other people will think about your choices? Or the choices of your partner, your children, your siblings - or anyone else, for fear that there's a 'guilt by association' issue?

If the answer is 'yes', ask yourself why.

"They might think I'm nuts!"

"They might think I'm awful!"

"They might think I'm (fill in the blank)!"

And your point is................???

Chances are, they won't. Because really, people aren't spending all that much time thinking about what we do. I mean, do you sit around for countless hours worrying about everyone else's decisions? I doubt it.

Sure, maybe you give them a passing thought now and then. Perhaps you even chat with other people about it. But do you really spend loads of time being preoccupied with other people's business? Not likely. (And if you do, it means you're probably doing it to avoid looking at your own life, your own unhappiness and what needs to change.)

Even more importantly, so what if they do think you're nuts or awful or (fill in the blank again)? Anyone who really knows you and really cares about you isn't gonna give a rat's @$$ what you do.

People who want to judge you are just being arrogant, forgetting that they aren't perfect and forgetting that they're probably doing things about which others might have a comment or two to make.

Those people's self-righteousness attitudes don't deserve your wasted time and energy.

Besides, even if you tried to live your life based on what everyone else thinks, you'd never get it right anyway. You'd get some of it right with some of the people some of the time. But there would always be a lot of people who'd be thinking you were doing it wrong because everyone is going to have a different view of things from others.

So you might as well not bother trying to make them all happy, and just worry about pleasing yourself.

After all, that's the only way you're ever going to find your bliss, be fulfilled, feel happy, explore and discover who you really are and who you're meant to be. Do you suppose you'll be on your deathbed someday, wishing you'd spent more time trying to dance to everyone else's tune? Do you suppose

those people will be on their deathbeds, thinking about you, your life and choices, and wishing you'd done things their way?

More likely, they'll see the error of their ways and be wishing they'd been more tolerant, less judgemental, allowed people to thrive and grow and just BE.

So if you're just going to end up causing yourself and a lot of other people nothing but deathbed distress, perhaps you'll want to start now and just look after yourself, doing what you want, doing what you think is right.

It's the best chance you've got to be happy, to be the best YOU that you can be, 'cause at the end of the day - and at the end of your life - what else is there that's worth the effort?

45. Don't reduce your dreams to fit your reality now. Expand your reality now to fit your dreams.

The whole point of having dreams is to do your best to achieve them. They allow you to think outside the box, to create goals for yourself that will enhance your life when you reach them. They allow you the freedom to create a fulfilling life that will bring you and your family happiness.

If dreams are supposed to do all that, how can any of it happen if you don't dream in a way that is bigger than your life is at the moment?

If your only dreams are to get a job you like better than the current one, or to pay off your credit cards, or to take a family holiday every year, then the most you can hope for is the job you like better, the credit cards to be paid off and the family holiday every year.

If you're not thinking about any more than that, you're not trying for any more than that. And if you're not trying for any more than that, you won't get any more than that. Life will be about plodding along, day after day, never knowing what great things you could achieve, what adventures you could have, or just how far you could really go.

We have imaginations. We are creative beings. Even if you're not creative in the traditional sense (i.e. art, music etc.), you still have the ability to create your own world, your own life. You are still able to carve out a life for yourself that makes you happy, that you find to be fulfilling and rewarding.

If that job you like, with no debts and a family holiday leave you feeling fulfilled and blissful, then that's great. More power to you. But if you find yourself sometimes being a bit wistful, wishing for that big house in the country, those exotic travels, the pursuit of hobbies that you think you can't afford in time or money, or if there is anything else you wish you could do or try, then there's a door with a dream on the other side of it.

Whether or not you choose to open that door is entirely up to you because you are the creator of your life, the master of your destiny, the weaver of your own dreams. No one but you can make them come true.

If you restrict your dreams by thinking you will only ever achieve the mundane, the usual, the average, then that's exactly what you'll get. But if you lift yourself out of what you already have and you allow yourself to imagine the possibilities, your life will begin to open up, to blossom and unfold in a way that begins to take you down new and exciting roads.

Dreams don't cost anything. They just ask to be heard, to be acknowledged. And what they give you in return will be amazing.

Go on. Open that door. And see where it leads you. It can only be somewhere wonderful.

46. There's nothing quite like a delicious little cuddle.

I was just out in my English country garden this morning, enjoying the birds' cheerful singing (with English accents, of course). As I mentioned in a recent post, I've been feeding and loving one of the cats in the village whose 'parents' can't be bothered with her and she's been chucked out, left to fend for herself. So as has become our routine, she was waiting for me on the mat outside the door when I went downstairs for a cup of tea.

As I sat at the table on the patio, scrawling a few thoughts in a notebook, I listened to her purr appreciatively while she wolfed down her food. Immediately upon finishing, she gave me that familiar look, asking if she could sit on my lap.

In a heartbeat, she was cuddled up in my arms, the thick softness of my dressing gown making a perfect little nest for her. With tiny feet kneading away, she purred even louder, rubbing the top of her head against me lovingly.

She pressed her thin little body into my chest as if she just couldn't get close enough. She and I are both very affectionate by nature, so I understand how she must be feeling.

It's a bit chilly this morning and her tiny ears were cold against my neck. Poor little darling, she just wants some love, some food and a warm home. Is that so much to ask?

I was only too happy to sit there with her for a while, holding her, loving her, and giving her some of the cuddles that I long to give my children and grandchildren in Canada. I sat there, asking The Universe to please make it possible for me to spend lots of time with them again, for us not to be separated like this all the time. It is the same request, day after day, moment after moment that I'm missing them and wishing I could be with them.

My situation is complicated, but then I suppose that's only fitting, as I, too, am complicated. Clearly, I am meant to be in this country, at least for now, and they are all meant to be in Calgary. I accept that, and all the learning that goes with it. I suppose each of us has lessons to learn from this separation.

In the meantime, I give this little kitty lots of love and cuddles because she needs them and I have them to give.

Do you know anyone who could use some cuddles? Just a bit of affection? Is there someone who needs a hug? Someone who feels isolated or abandoned, and could stand to know someone cares?

You've got nothing to lose because when you're giving cuddles, you're getting some back at the same time.

So go on. Give someone an affectionate little cuddle today. Or perhaps a big one. You'll both feel better for it.

47. Good day! Or is it? That's entirely up to you!

What kind of day are you having? I hope it's been a good one so far. But if it's been less than wonderful up until now, the rest of it can be much better – if that's what you want.

I know what it's like to have days in which absolutely everything seems to go wrong. And it's extra nasty when you've got the weight of the world on your shoulders, just to top it all off. But you can turn it around.

Just stop. Take a deep breath and let it out slowly. Don't think about all the things that went wrong, or all the miseries that are weighing you down.

Right here, in this moment, just empty that stuff out of your head and think about now.

Re-set your intention to have a harmonious life. Re-set your intention to be happy, to relax, to feel peaceful. Re-set your intention to focus on the positives and diminish the negatives.

If your relationship is in trouble, your job is on the line – or you don't have one and you need one – if you're worried about someone who is critically ill (and that 'someone' might even be you), just put it all out of your head for this moment, right here, right now.

Just close your eyes and listen to the sounds around you. Breathe deeply and evenly, focusing on letting all the tension drain out of your body.

You can't fix your relationship or your job right this minute. You can't alter those Bigger Picture miseries in the next few moments. Or even by the end of the day.

But you can continually put yourself back in a calm and focused state of mind, focusing on *now*, this very moment, and nothing else.

If you keep focusing on *now*, being mindful of every present moment, and only dealing what is right there in front of you to be dealt with in that very moment, suddenly life is not overwhelming. You will no longer feel as though you're handling the whole mountain at once, but rather, this small step that's right there waiting to be taken.

Imagine a huge buffet table set with loads and loads of plates and platters all filled with food. And you are a four-year-old child standing there, expected to eat it all.

Overwhelming? Absolutely. Daunting? Definitely. Impossible? Completely. Ready to give up before you begin? Most assuredly.

Be that little kid. Close your eyes. Take a deep breath and relax as you exhale. Open your eyes and look at one small plate. Then take one little piece of food off that plate and nibble on it. That is your present moment managed. Never mind the rest. The other moments will follow one at a time. They'll take care of themselves if you don't try to stuff them all in at once and drive yourself nuts.

And as for all the things that just seem to go wrong in a day, that's part of life. Let them go and start thinking about all the things that went right up until this moment. And as the rest of your day unfolds, keep focusing on what goes right. If there are any more glitches, just stop, do not let yourself get bent out of shape. Take a deep breath, think about all the things that are right, that are okay, that are just fine – and move on to the next moment.

If you keep focusing on what goes right and ignore or let go of what goes wrong, your day is guaranteed to improve. It's entirely up to you.

Go on. Have a wonderful day.

48. **Do not diminish your pain, your accomplishments or your life because of anyone else's.**

We've all got a story. We've all had difficulties, heartache and loss. We've all suffered. Certainly, some of us suffer more than others. Some roads are an awful lot bumpier than others. Some of us know heartache and pain way too well.

And when you're in the midst of it, who cares if someone has had more troubles? What does it matter that someone else had a worse life, a more abused childhood, a more tragic background?

What matters is that you hurt, too. In that moment, you're the one who is suffering. Don't discount it and say you have no right to complain or to feel bad. Don't diminish your own pain and tell yourself it's not as important as anyone else's. It's not a competition.

What's most important is finding a way to handle your pain and troubles, finding acceptance, peace, problem-resolution - whatever needs to happen in order for you to continue moving forward in your life and not letting the bumpy bits slow you down.

We've all got talents. We've all got abilities, skills, gifts and strengths. Do not diminish yours and treat them as though they are not as valuable as those of other people. Do not wipe out your accomplishments, your creativity, your uniqueness, just because you believe (mistakenly) that other people's gifts are bigger, better, more than yours. No one can be you. No one can give exactly what you give.

If you don't know what your talents are, poke around and find out. Try new things, or ask other people because sometimes we don't see our own gifts and abilities but others do. Your friends might point out something you're really good at that you hadn't thought about in that way.

Everything about you is valid. Everything about you is worthy of being acknowledged. Whether it is your pain or your triumph, your disappointment or your joy - or anything in between. It is valid and worthy because it is part of you. There is nothing about you that needs to be compared with anyone else, for you and your own experiences are unique.

And there never has been and never will be another you. Celebrate how special you are.

49. On fearing change

Recently, I've had a few people telling me that they would love to make changes in their lives but they're afraid of the fallout. They're afraid of the repercussions with family or friends who would not approve or whose own lives would, in some way, be changed, too.

I understand how this feels. I've been in those shoes myself on many occasions.

But I've learned what other people think is none of my business - and what I do is none of theirs - even if they are affected by my choices. They are still my choices to make, as I am the only one walking my path and I must follow it as I see fit, for I'm the only one who has to live in my skin and deal with the consequences of my actions - or inactions.

And there is one thing I know for sure: It's best to keep moving forward, no matter what.

When change happens, it is because it was needed. We don't always have to understand why or how, but we can be sure it was necessary. It can be the catalyst for others to change, too, not just ourselves.

Perhaps when we stay stuck, when we choose to hold back from doing what we really want or need to do, we are also holding others back, too.

Perhaps we are meant to make those changes in order to allow others to progress.

It's like clearing out the weeds in the garden and making room for seeds to grow, or plants to spread and thrive. Or perhaps opening the cage door and letting the bird fly.

If you're worrying about the reactions of other people, or the effect that your choices will have on them, consider this: Do you suppose they would want you to be miserable? Do you suppose they would like to know that you're unhappy, and that they're the ones who are keeping you that way?

If the answer to either of those questions is 'yes', then frankly, those people's opinions are not worth another thought. If they would really prefer you to be miserable, then it makes no sense to care at all what they think.

And if the answer to those questions is 'no', then you have no need to worry about the fallout. Anyone who truly loves and cares about you will accept you as you are, and will accept whatever you need to do in order to progress. They might have to be dragged kicking and screaming into it if your changes affect them a lot, but that's okay. Time passes, people adjust, things settle down.

We are not born to stay the same. Otherwise, we would not grow and our bodies would not change. We would not have developed technology, methods of communication or long-distance travel. We would not be thinking, creating beings. We would not learn new hobbies, write new music, develop new theories.

Change can be a little frightening sometimes. Or even a lot. But so what? Is that a reason to avoid it? When you resist it, that's what hurts. That's what makes it painful. It's best to accept it, go with the flow, embrace it as a constant in your life and change your attitude about it. See it as something that is good, that keeps the energy around you vibrant and healthy.

If you want something to change, then it **needs** to change. Whether you like it or not, whether anyone else likes it or not. And if you refuse to do it, then other things will begin to change anyway and the whole process will be more difficult. You can choose the easier way - with acceptance and positivity - or the harder way, with resistance and fear.

Sometimes, the toughest choices are the best ones. What looks like an easy way out is often a trap that lands you in quicksand. It may, indeed, be difficult to move on, to leave people behind, to start over, to find a new way to deal with an old problem, or to go in a new direction - whatever that means to you - but if you're not happy where you are, or if you know you'd be happier after that change, then listen to the little voice inside you.

It is your Higher Self, speaking to you with its Divine wisdom, urging you to move forward with your life.

Sure, staying stuck and frustrated is an option. But why would you choose that over growth and happiness?

And consider this: Perhaps some of those people about whom you're worrying are just waiting for you - or someone - to make the first move. Perhaps they're aching for change but are also afraid of the repercussions. Perhaps they're afraid of what you'll think of their changes.

Sticking your head in the sand isn't gonna make your desire for change go away. And it isn't gonna get you where you want to be, if that isn't where you are right now.

The people who really love you will understand that, and will support you until you get there. And you never know. By opening the door to your own happiness, you might just be doing the same for them.

50. If you say it, mean it. If you mean it, prove it.

I shouldn't really have to elaborate on that title. It speaks for itself. But as I'm here, what the heck!

"If you say it, mean it." How do you feel when people tell you things, and then you find out they aren't true? Or they've made promises to you, but then forget or just don't follow through and keep them?

It's one thing if someone has a really good reason for not following through.

For example, "I was in a car accident that day." But it's quite another to find out that people have made things up just to impress you, or they've exaggerated, or they've promised to do something that they had little or no intention of doing.

I'm sure you've been on the receiving end of incidents like these. And there's a good chance you weren't too impressed on those occasions, and that your ability to trust those people again was somewhat dented and banged up.

No doubt you wouldn't want to treat others that way, when you didn't like it yourself.

So it's easy. When you open your mouth and words are going to come out, make sure they're words you really mean. Be honourable. Follow through. Don't tell people they can count on you and then leave them hanging - unless you have a very good reason for doing it.

Don't make up stuff just to impress. Your truth is perfect as it is. Don't turn it into a lie, because that just puts a big, black blotch on your spirit - and on your relationship with the person who heard the lie.

"If you mean it, prove it." Think about those televangelists who were caught having affairs and misappropriating funds. Think about the priests, teachers, lawyers and others who have been caught abusing their authority. What do you think about people who have double standards? How do you feel about that?

If you're going to be a smoker, don't tell others not to do it. If you're going to be a couch potato, don't tell me I ought to get more exercise. If you're gonna talk the talk, you've gotta walk the walk or no one will take you seriously. Hypocrisy isn't gonna get you very far in life. Not if you want to have solid relationships - including the one you have with yourself.

If you've changed your mind often enough that even you don't trust yourself to follow through any more, how can you expect anyone else to trust you? If you've backed down from your convictions a bunch of times, and chickened out of standing up for yourself, how can you expect anyone else to have any faith in you?

It's about having integrity. Both personally and professionally, that goes a hell of a lot further than hypocrisy and cowardice.

If you know you may not live up to the words that are about to come out of your mouth, do yourself and any potential listener a favour: Leave them where they are.

51. Little kids know some pretty cool stuff.

Little kids have it straight. I'm talking about really little kids, like about 3-4 years old.

You never have to wonder where you stand with them. They're completely honest. They cry when they're sad or they hurt. They yell when they're angry. They just tell it like it is, full stop.

If they don't like the food you prepare, they'll tell you. If they don't like your new haircut, they'll tell you. If they think your bum looks big in that, they'll tell you. They're just completely honest. They don't have a clue about being politically correct, and there's no need to lie or back-pedal because to them, there's no such thing as a social faux pas.

And they're so good at equality. They don't have a clue about social status. They don't understand about money, or that Little Johnny's doctor daddy is considered by many to be somehow superior to Little Susie's shelf-stocking one. They'll offer a sticky little handful of sweets to a 'poor kid' as easily as to a 'rich kid' because to them, a kid is a kid is a kid.

And for the same reason, they'll play with a green kid, a purple kid, an orange kid or a striped kid. They'll play with a kid who speaks in some bizarre language that they don't understand, or to a kid who can't speak at all, or the kid who "looks funny". Hey, if there's another kid in that waiting room or on the playground, it's all good. Let's play.

They don't know the doctor is extremely busy and hasn't got time to hear about their new pets, their new crayons, or how little Mary threw up in Sunday school last week and got some on her shoes. They have no idea that when they want to sit and tell him these things, he has the opportunity to remember why he became a doctor in the first place.

They don't know they shouldn't ask the lady in the wheelchair why she has only one leg. They don't know about discrimination or pity or other such unpleasantries in life; they just ask because they're curious, not because they see her as anything other than a lady with one leg.

Little kids are uncomplicated. If there's a problem, they don't bring up a bunch of other ones while you're trying to address just the one. They like to follow the KISS rule: Keep It Simple, Stupid.

They stick up for their best friends. They invite everybody to their birthday parties. They remember if you were nice to them. They love to show you their bedrooms and all their toys and stuff because they have nothing to hide; they have no secrets.

When they're tired, they fall asleep. They don't care if it's at the dinner table, in a restaurant, at Aunt Sylvia's 75th birthday party or at the playground. When they're hungry, they make sure everyone in a 92-mile-radius knows it. When they're mad at you, they say so, right now, right here, in your face, no holds barred. They'll tell you exactly why, point blank, nice and clear, so there can be no question.

In such honesty, such clarity, and such purity, there is great wisdom. We could all stand to be more like little kids. They have all the answers that we spend a bunch of years forgetting, and the rest of our lives trying to remember.

52. Where are Ted and a blankie when you need them? Right under your nose.

Remember how easy it was to solve life's miseries when you were a kid? Okay, I'm not talking about the big horrible ones that many of us have experienced in toxic homes and that sort of thing, but your average bumps and bruises of childhood, being told 'no', or being sent to your room for some minor infraction, your best friend won't share toys or has gone to play with some other little kid...

You knew just how to fix those booboos. You had your very best pal, "Ted" - you know, the ratty, old, worn stuffed bear - or a reasonable facsimile. "Ted" was always there, ready to be dragged around, squished too hard, cried on, and then left with the dust bunnies under the bed when you forgot why you were crying in the first place. And he never even minded, bless him.

Or you had your blankie. Tattered and threadbare, it could probably stand up by itself unless your mama peeled it out from under you while you were sleeping and stuffed it in the washing machine. When the world was being mean to you, you could grab your blankie and retreat by curling up in your favourite chair or in your bed until you fell asleep or perhaps something else got your attention.

Then you grew up. Life got harder. Problems were bigger. That frustrated little kid who just wants to cry is still inside you on your bad days. That little kid just wants to stamp a foot and run for Ted and Blankie.

But they're nowhere to be found. Who knows where they went, but bless them, they took all your secrets with them, never to be shared.

So you and the little kid inside just carry on, the little kid wanting to burst into tears or run away (or both), but you say no, we have to stay put. The

129

weight of the world is on your shoulders but there's no Ted to talk to, no blankie for comfort.

Then you end up at the kitchen table of some kindly old lady, perhaps a neighbour or an aunt who shoves a cuppa tea at you, saying it'll put everything right. It's like a big hug, she says, nice and warm and comforting.

You're not the type to open up and tell people stuff. Oh, no, you couldn't do that! Not that she's asking. She just wants you to have a cuppa tea.

So you're happy to sit there, and drink your tea, and the kindly old lady doesn't say much. She's kinda like Ted that way.

Then a few words escape your lips. And a few more and a few more and your tea disappears while you find yourself telling her what's wrong.

And how cool is that? She was right. By the time you finish that tea, you feel better. It was just like a big hug, nice and warm and comforting - like your blankie. You haven't solved all your problems, by any means. But maybe you've got a new perspective. Maybe things don't seem so bad. Or maybe you see that you don't have to fix everything right now.

All that matters in that moment is that you feel better. You can face those problems again. Maybe even tackle one or two in the morning.

Thank heaven for the Teds in our lives, who so willingly share their blankies with us.

53. You can't help someone who doesn't want it.

When it comes to offering help, there are three kinds of people in the world. There are those who can help themselves, but who sometimes need a little boost along the way. There are those who cannot help themselves, so you help wherever possible. And then there are those who will not help themselves and they want you to do it for them.

The challenge lies in trying to figure out who's who. And in not wasting your time and energy on that third group.

A few years ago, through the course of my work, I made an online 'friend'. A rather difficult and lonely man, he relied on me quite heavily for support and encouragement, which I've always been happy to give. It required a lot of patience on my part at times but I did my best to lift his spirits and to be friendly with him.

He was hard work, to say the least. No matter what I've said, in these few years he has continued to be as negative and stuck as ever. That was certainly his choice, and as long as it wasn't hurting me to carry on trying to cheer him up and help him, I was happy to continue.

So for these years, I've been able to look past his self-pitying misery, and I kept hoping that someday, something I would say might make a difference, and he would see that he could be happier if he just bothered to try. In hopes that he might find a more positive view of his situation, my blog posts have sometimes been aimed at him, but I don't think he ever saw it, even though he read it every day.

Recently, he ordered me to do something. I ignored his demand but he wouldn't leave it alone. He did it a few times, becoming more insistent and even writing "grrrr - or else!" the last time.

I was more than just a little annoyed. This was not the first time I'd heard this kind of thing from him, and I repeated what I'd said on similar occasions in the past. I told him that was the quickest way to get me to do the opposite of what he wanted. And I said nobody tells me what to do.

I even stuck a little smiley face there, and then chatted about the rest of my day, in an effort to make my point without appearing to be angry.

Then he fired back a terrible insult, telling me to stay single because no man could put up with my selfishness.

And there was another comment after that, which was so unbearably cruel, I simply could not believe my eyes. He tore at an extremely painful wound in my life, ripped it wide open - and worse, he has no idea about the circumstances or anything at all to do with the situation that he was using in an effort to hurt me, and/or to get me to do what he wanted. Yet he saw fit to insult me and to make horrible and untrue assumptions that were just downright nasty.

And all because I stood up for myself and refused to be told what to do.

That little voice inside me said it was time to walk away. But I was faced with a dilemma. What about loving people unconditionally? What about forgiveness?

Well, it didn't take long for me to realise that none of that is a problem. I still believe that there is a perfect divine spirit behind the hurtful words of the man. I can still love the spirit, and forgive the man. But forgiveness doesn't mean his behaviour is okay. It only means I have no interest in dragging around the pain of this incident.

Okay, so I can still love the spirit and forgive the man. So why walk away?

Because of that little voice inside. The one that says he crossed a line - again. The one that says this time he went too far. The one that has noticed other inappropriate comments escalating recently, but I continued to give him the benefit of the doubt because I really wanted to help him. The one that says this is a much bigger, deeper issue than it seems on the surface, and if I don't put a stop to it now, I'm just going back for more.

I have ignored and forgiven many inappropriate comments that he's made in the years I've known him but I'd always thought he was relatively harmless. Until now. That little voice is screaming at me.

So I am listening - because if there's anything I've learned in this very difficult life, it is that the little voice never lies.

That little voice knew this man is one of the ones who refuses to help himself.

Finally, I saw that despite my best efforts all these years, he has showed no interest in helping himself, in healing, in improving his life. He was only interested in wallowing in his miseries, using my kindness to lift his spiritshere and there, draining my energy to make himself feel better because he couldn't be bothered to do it for himself.

And on top of that, he would spew venom at me on occasion.

Well, it is not my purpose on the planet to be anyone's toxic waste dump. Heaven knows there are plenty of people out there who appreciate my friendship and my help, and I'm happy to give them loads of both. I have no interest in wasting any more time or energy on someone who refuses to help himself, or to respect me.

I was a bit slow in spotting it, but better late than never. And now, the time and energy that I used to spend on him will be better used to help someone who appreciates my efforts.

54. Don't push the river. BE the river.

I know. You want it now.

Actually, if you had your druthers, you'd have had it last week. Whatever 'it' is. It's going to make you happy. It's going to relieve the burden. It's going to take away the stress. It's going to give you peace.

So you want 'it' now.

Impatience is not a happy thing. It's an aching, frustrating, miserable thing. It's the quickest way to make time slow down and in the nastiest way possible because it makes every clock tease and torment you. Every day, every week taunts you with "I won again!" and you feel increasingly disappointed as time seems to drag even slower.

Impatience makes you unhappy. It adds a burden. It gives you stress. And it does not allow peace. It only gives you more of the miseries you're hoping to escape.

The more you think about how slowly time is going, the longer it seems to take, and the more impatient you become. Then time seems slower still, and the whole chicken-and-egg process gets worse, and before long, you're just this side of tearing your hair out by the roots.

Stop. Take a couple of deep breaths. Refocus. Understand that by choosing to focus on 'hurry up' thoughts, you're just asking for more impatient feelings, which will only bring you more misery. And that's a pretty huge waste of your precious energy.

Calm down. Remember that time keeps ticking along at the same rate of speed, hour after hour, day after day, week after week, no matter how you feel about it. It's like a river that just keeps flowing. You toss a stick in it, and it will bob and bounce along with the water, steadily, continuously, winding its way to wherever it's heading. Nothing makes it go faster. Nothing makes it go slower. But it keeps moving.

Your feelings are a direct result of your thoughts, which you can control if you choose to do it. Whatever you're thinking will influence how you're feeling. Immediately. Every time. Always. Because you're in control of what you're thinking about, you are always able to control your feelings.

So you have a choice to make. Do you want to feel even unhappier, more burdened and stressed? Or do you want to aim for that peace you think you can only feel when you get 'it'?

You can have happiness now. You can have a lighter burden and less stress now. You can feel peaceful now. In this moment, this very moment that you're standing in right now, accept all things about your situation. Accept that this is how things are, right here, right now. That doesn't mean you won't fix it or it won't change or improve. Just acknowledge that while that's going on, you accept how it is now.

Never mind what's missing. Never mind what's not right. Instead, be grateful. Think about abundance. Think about what you have. Think about the blessings, what works, what's right in your life, in your circumstances, in your environment.

When you spend your time focusing on the abundance and the positives in your life, it is impossible to be upset about what's missing. You cannot feel the peace and gratitude of abundance at the same time as you're feeling frustration and lack.

When you're focused on abundance and gratitude, you will feel happiness. You will feel less burdened and less stress. You will feel a beautiful sense of peace. It'll be much easier for you to feel content and patient about waiting for 'it'.

Don't push the river. Appreciate its beauty. Appreciate how it sparkles in the sun while it nurtures plants, fish and other little critters. Appreciate the way it twists and winds through the earth, not knowing where it's going and not caring, meandering gently, not needing to rush and discover its destination because it knows it's getting there anyway.

Don't push the river. Be the river. And you will have your peace - now.

55. Think yourself into Wellness.

When we're ill, whether from something minor or something serious, it's easy to think about how miserable we're feeling because it can affect so much of what we do.

It's a challenge to think positive, healthy thoughts when we're feeling really unwell. You might just feel like a big liar, telling yourself you feel wonderful when you feel absolutely horrible, so you give up right away.

But the more we can do thinking positive, healing thoughts, the better our chances of feeling well - and in fact, of being well - because we produce positive energy which can only be of benefit to us on all levels.

Our thoughts produce energy. For those of you who think that's a load of rubbish, talk to the scientists who have proven it with their gadgetry.

Positive thoughts produce hundreds of times more energy than negative ones. Also proven with science.

If you're still not convinced, how about a little "let's pretend"? Let's pretend that changing your thoughts would make you feel better. I'm not talking about an instant cure, although that would be a pretty cool trick. Let's pretend but within reason, okay?

Let's pretend that if you shoved all thoughts of illness, disease, and not feeling well right out of your head, you would feel better. Whatever that means specifically is irrelevant. Let's pretend that whenever a thought about your pain, your prognosis, your diagnosis, your treatment plan, the doctor's opinions about the course of the disease or anything related wanders through your head, replacing it with thoughts of healing would make it happen.

It should be easy to say all that stuff if you're just pretending, right? It's saying it and meaning it that's a bit tricky. Sounds pretty good, right? And it doesn't even cost anything.

Okay, so what have you got to lose by trying? What if it works? Wouldn't that be very cool?

As a hypnotist, I've seen some pretty miraculous things to do with the power of the mind. And then there's multiple personality disorder. Sometimes, a person suffering from this condition will have a personality who has diabetes - with blood tests to prove it, sugars going crazy, needing insulin injections etc. - but when the other personalities are in control, there isn't a sign of it in the body.

Whether that's deliberate or not isn't the point. In fact, that it isn't deliberate actually helps to prove my point. If the body can do all that by itself when directed by some unconscious or subconscious part of the mind, just imagine what we could do if we took control and directed it on a conscious level!

So you're feeling miserable. How are you supposed to talk yourself into feeling well?

I'm not suggesting it's quite that simple but making the effort is important and like anything else we have to learn, it gets easier with practice.

Begin by not talking about your disease. Sure, people will ask how you are, and if you want to give those closest to you an honest update, be quick about it. For all other people, if they're not directly affected by your situation, tell them you're fine. Or that you were ill but you're now recovering.

If it's too much for you to tell yourself you're completely healthy, you can at least replace all thoughts of illness with thoughts like, "I'm healing." Or "I'm recovering." "I'm getting better."

As those thoughts come more readily, you may begin to find it easier to say you are already well and healed.

Let's pretend it works, because pretending removes your current reality and the attached emotions. It gives you a bit of breathing room, which allows new information and new feelings to come in. There are numerous cases of people spontaneously healing terminal illness, just by insisting on believing that they were perfectly healthy. Bearing that in mind, there is really no excuse not to give their method a shot.

So go on. Give it a try but remember, it takes time to get rid of old habits, and to develop new ones so be patient with yourself and keep pretending that these thoughts will make you feel better - whatever that might mean. There's every reason to believe they will.

56. We believe we create intention. But intention creates us.

Intention is the source of all creation. Generally, we think of intention as consciously focusing on a desire, an aim, a goal, and not letting anything stop us from achieving it. But if you're not one of those 'dog-with-a-bone' people who sink their teeth into something and refuses to let go until they get it, don't despair. As it turns out, intention does not originate with our conscious thoughts - or with willpower.

"In the universe there is an immeasurable, indescribable force which shamans call intent, and absolutely everything that exists in the entire cosmos is attached to intent by a connecting link." - Carlos Castaneda

Imagine that. Intention is not something we can actively create within ourselves. Intention is everywhere. It is a force that is inside us, around us, flowing through us. It is there for us to use at any time by making and maintaining that link. This is much easier to do than using sheer willpower, which can be fickle as it is closely tied to our emotions.

Einstein and his cohorts knew that particles are not at the source of creation - i.e. particles do not create more particles. The Source of creation is intention, a pure energy that vibrates at such a high rate of speed that it cannot be measured. It is invisible and without form, and at our Source, we were that energy.

At the moment of conception, everything about how you would look and what your personality would be, everything that makes you 'you' was set in motion by intention. Whether physical or non-physical, intention is the energy that activated your potential. The only way you can deactivate it is by breaking that link, and you do this when you believe that you are separate from intention.

We can see intention at work everywhere in nature. Every seed intends to grow into a specific plant. Every animal, fish, bird and insect intends to grow, survive, reproduce, and create the existence that was intended for it. And every one of them does it without thinking about it or questioning it.

Therefore, nothing in nature is ever disconnected from intention. Nothing, that is, except humans with our intelligence which allows us to question everything, including our intention, and our very existence. We've created a separateness for ourselves that disconnects us in the form of ego. Rather than seeing that we are all living in this same energy field of intention, we have removed ourselves from it and believe that each of us is a separate entity in the universe. We believe we create intention. But intention creates us.

Ego separates us by identifying who and what we are on a very earthly, human level. It defines us by what we do, by the opinions of others, and by what we have. It keeps us feeling separated from everything that's missing in our lives, from everyone else, and from the Divine Source of all Creation ("God", "Goddess", or whatever term you prefer).

"Intent is a force that exists in the universe. When sorcerers (those who live of the Source) beckon intent, it comes to them and sets up the path for attainment, which means that sorcerers always accomplish what they set out to do." - Carlos Castaneda

The link between us, and the force that is intention, comes from connection with Spirit. As long as you allow ego to do your thinking for you, you will remain disconnected from Spirit, from Source, and from the power of intention.

You know that feeling you get when you feel inspired? When something lights a fire under you, and you feel a sense of purpose, you're energised and you're just itching to get at whatever it is that you feel driven to do in that moment of inspiration? Think of being inspired as being "in-spirited".

In that wonderful moment of inspiration, that is when you're connected to Source. That is when you connect with intention. Leaving ego out of the equation keeps you linked with Source and feeling in-spirited.

Okay, so intention is not about dogged determination that is only accessible to those with a serious stubborn streak. Intention is everywhere, anyone can access it by linking with Source, and it's easier to do that, than it is to use willpower.

So where do you sign up? How do you make that link? How do you become a 'sorcerer'?

You begin by believing that we are not separate beings, but that we are all connected by Source. When you believe this, you can see that we're also connected to everything we desire, to all we hope to be, to do, to accomplish. In aligning - or realigning - ourselves in this way, we reactivate the power of intention that has always been there, waiting for us to return to the in-spirited paths that were intended for us from the moment of conception.

57. Oops. I crashed and burned. Again.

When I was a kid, I remember my mother telling me about an expression, "When you need something done, ask a busy person."

I thought that was nuts. If that person is busy, why ask him/her to do even more?? Seemed downright disrespectful to me.

But then I grew up. On numerous occasions, I saw "not-busy people" being not busy. I heard them say they had stuff to do but didn't feel like doing it. And it didn't get done.

I saw "busy people" being busy. I heard them say they had stuff to do and they did it without saying much about whether or not it needed doing. And sometimes they said they didn't feel like doing it. But it got done anyway.

I've been a very busy person in my life. With five children, a lot of single parenting - at one point even juggling five part-time jobs to try to make ends meet - with really terrible health issues and a whole mess of personal problems thrown in, stuff always got done. I have a significant case of A.D.D. (Attention Deficit Disorder) but I've learned to live with it, to work around it, and am extremely organised and responsible and I get things done.

Whatever the reason for it, I'm just a very busy person. But I enjoy it. I need loads of intellectual and creative stimulation. I get bored very easily. My mind is always racing with the millions of things I want to do. I'm always thinking, wondering, analysing, creating.

It is very difficult for me to slow down. And even harder for me to stop. I live in overdrive and don't notice it - I suppose because of the A.D.D. I suppose it's really A.D.H.D., although the 'hyperactive' part is not physical with me, but it is very much on the mental level.

Because I'm always burning the candle at both ends - and in the middle - I don't notice when I'm running on empty. So I keep going till I'm running on fumes. Then I notice, but I'm having such a good time doing things, being busy, creating stuff, the hyperactivity in my brain doesn't allow me notice until I crash and burn.

Oops.

I used to keep going on crash and burn. Don't ask me how, but I did it. I reckon it's because I had no choice, especially as a single parent with too many "film-worthy" dramatic circumstances that required my energy and attention.

At least now, I stop when I get there. But the lesson for me has been to stop before reaching that point! Finally, I learned that lesson. Sort of.

A few weeks back, I saw crash-and-burn coming. I wrote about it here, too. I had a plan. I'd been working for 18+ hours a day, virtually every day, for the past few years. I enjoy what I do, so I didn't notice it was too much work and virtually no play.

But yippee for me, I realised I was on overload, and I made a plan to spend a few hours every morning on 'playtime' before beginning work.

So I get a point for having reached that conclusion - it was a very big deal for me.

But I just had to finish this and get that done, and meet a couple of deadlines and then I was going to start with my new plan. Honest.

Oops.

I hit crash and burn again.

The old tapes played in my head. "But what about this healing night I'm supposed to do? What about my Tuesday evening group this week? I don't want to disappoint anyone! And what about my belly dancing class?"

Well, I'm happy to say I didn't play those tapes too long. They were pretty quickly replaced with "I must look after myself. If I don't, I'll be no good to anyone. And I'm not responsible for anyone else's feelings so I cannot worry about people being disappointed. And I certainly shouldn't be jeopardising my health in order to keep them from feeling that way."

So I get big points for that.

I knew, too, that anyone who truly cares about me would understand that if I'm not well, I should be resting. I knew that they would support that, and would want me to take care of myself. In years gone by, none of that would have crossed my mind but I value and respect myself now, when long ago, I

did not. And because I care about myself and respect myself, I understand that others also care about me and respect me, too.

Another point, please.

I'm happy about the fact that I recognised a 'crash and burn' on the way and made a plan to prevent it. That's a big step in the right direction (although I could have done it a little sooner).

And I'm happy about the fact that I slid past the old tapes pretty quickly, and I've been feeling really good about resting, resting, resting, resting - and resting for the past several days.

I'm really happy about the fact that I passed the test about walking the walk if you're going to talk the talk.

Next time, I'll start walking a little sooner. Okay, a lot sooner. In fact, it starts with putting my plan into practice, having some balance in my life with some play time, and limiting myself to a maximum of 12 hours' work every day. Over 7 days, that's still 84 hours a week so I can hardly beat myself up for being a slacker.

I promise I won't even let myself get to the 'running on empty' part, let alone on fumes or crashing and burning. Will you make the same promise for yourself?

58. Arguing is a good thing. Until...

There are a few people on the planet who seem to enjoy arguing. You know the kind...the ones who seem to say black just because you said white, and as soon as you say "Okay, black", then they say, "No, wait, it's white." They argue just for the sake of it. Heaven only knows what's gone on in their lives to make them spew such hostility, and of course there's a huge power play going on, so there's obviously something that's happened which has left them feeling a need for control.

You will never win an argument with those people because they're not arguing about an issue, standing up for themselves, or acting on principle. They won't hear a thing you say and you can't make any valid points because the issue doesn't matter in the least. They just want to manipulate you into being upset or into giving up, so they feel powerful.

Then there's the other kind of argument. The kind that you can quickly see is going nowhere. Arguments - or at least disagreements - are a fact of life. It is inevitable that we won't see eye-to-eye with others, and sometimes emotions get thrown into the mix and presto - your very own argument.

There's nothing wrong with arguing. What's important, however, is how you do it. Is it with closed ears and a closed mind? Your way is the right way, full stop? Your feelings are the only ones that matter, or they matter more than the other person's - is that your attitude?

Or is it with a listening heart? That is, with compassion, so you're doing your best to see the situation from the other person's perspective? That's the best way to understand - and with understanding, you can find your way to resolution a whole lot quicker.

It's important to stay focused on the issue, and not let other ones get dragged into it. That's like trying to bake a cake, and then throwing in the ingredients for Sunday roast, a Caesar salad, and a full English breakfast all at once. The result would be pretty horrible, to say the least, and your cake will have been lost in the mess.

If this happens, take a 'time out' and come back to it later, whether it takes minutes, hours - or heaven forbid, days. But if the issue is that important to you, it needs to be discussed, no matter how much time has passed between the incident and the resolution. Ignoring it won't make it go away. It'll only create a distance between you and the other person.

It's also important to recognise when the argument is going nowhere. When it becomes clear that there is no progress, no forward movement, and for some reason, you're just stuck in a sort of "Yes it is" "No it isn't" "Yes it is" "No it isn't" situation.

If you see that you're getting nowhere and you must agree to disagree, then say so - and walk away. If you can see you're just not being understood, or if the Sunday roast and the "full English" have been thrown in, call for a time out and come back to clarify things later.

The point is, it may take only one person to start an argument, but it takes two for it to continue. As long as it is done appropriately and respectfully, while sticking to the issue at hand, and you're making progress toward mutual understanding, carry on.

But it's important to recognise the points at which it's becoming destructive, or at least unproductive.

When tempers flare or things get emotional, back off. Take a 'time out'. Think about what's happening. Then decide whether you can drop it where it lies, or if you'll need to continue at a later date.

59. Damn. Mother's Day. Again.

Today is Mother's Day. Well, in Canada, where I'm from, and in some other parts of the world. Over here in England, I've already been slammed with this occasion this year, as it happens earlier in the spring. In all the years I've been living in England, it's always been a bittersweet day for me, although I'm never sure which is in greater quantity, the bitter or the sweet.

There are no words to describe the love I feel for my children, and my grandchildren. There is no way to express my gratitude about having been given such precious gifts.

I was speaking with one of my daughters yesterday about how she's living her dream of being a mommy with little kids at home. I was a heartbeat away from being back in those days of my life. I slid right into the memories as easily as if they were the most comfortable old slippers.

I remember the very first flutters of a tiny little being inhabiting my body as it called, "Hello? Anybody out there?" The honest answer to that could only be yes, I was - and still am - very much 'out there' but somehow all of my children have survived their mother being nuts.

I remember breast-feeding and being a gnawed on like a teething ring as tiny razors poked their way through painful gums.

And years later, putting those little teeth under pillows with excited bedtime wonderings about what the Tooth Fairy would bring.

I remember my older children petting poor mommy who was sick whilst a new little sibling was tucked neatly inside her, wreaking havoc on her tummy.

I remember crayon on bedroom walls and furniture because there was all that blank space just screaming 'Draw on me!' I remember nail polish on mommy's chair, clothes and carpet because it was bright red and oh, so pretty!

I remember baking cookies with tiny hands helping. Baking cakes with little mouths wanting to lick the bowl. Making soup with a four-year-old son wanting to "sharpen the carrots".

I remember decorating a cake by writing "Happy Birthday" backwards so all the 7-year-olds at the party were amazed when I held a big mirror over the cake so they could see what it said.

I remember shocking my teenaged daughter when instead of candles, I put 16 lit cigarettes on her birthday cake. It was hilarious watching her and her boyfriend frantically putting them out so they could smoke them later. (Ew.)

I remember being upstairs, hearing 3-year-old Jacob say "I hate you!" to 3-year-old Willow downstairs (No, not twins, but 7-1/2 months apart). I called down, "That's not very nice!"

Silence. Then Willow's voice. "Mummy?"

"Yes?"

"Was that you?" she asked.

"Yes."

And Willow's priceless comment, "Oh. I thought it was God."

I remember being told one morning that it was "Ted's" birthday (Willow's stuffed bear and best pal). When she got home from school, she was surprised to find a birthday cake for him, complete with teddy bear paper hats, teddy bear paper plates, teddy bear napkins - the whole nine yards. After all, Ted was a member of the family. He used to get seat-belted into the car when I'd drop the children off at school, and he was there when I picked them up, and I gave an accounting of what he did that day with me. I must say, he was a very busy bear.

I remember being on a bus with two-year-old Amy, who hadn't seen her curly-haired, moustached daddy for six months, and on seeing an equally curly-haired, moustached man several seats behind us, she began yelling, "DADDY! DADDY!"

The woman next to him shot dagger looks at me, at him, at me, at him, while he shook his head frantically, no no no no NO! - before she practically dragged him off the bus by his ear at the next stop.

I've often wondered whatever happened after that...

I remember food fights in the kitchen, with hilarity and squealing, laughter and silliness - and I was often the one who started them.

I remember teaching my children nursery rhymes - well, my version of them - and then listening to frustrated stories of how the teacher or the day care ladies insisted, "That's not how they go..."

I remember being in hospital with one child or another for broken bones, or stitches, or seizures, or car accidents or suicide attempts or a suspected inoperable brain tumour, and hearing a chunk of my heart break with every one of those terrifying visits.

I remember the crushing knowledge that I couldn't give my children everything I wanted them to have, that my choices had caused them pain and disappointment when I tried so hard to make their lives magical and perfect. I remember feeling like a complete failure for letting them down, for not being able to fix everything, for not being able to protect them from all the miseries that life has thrown at them.

I remember watching my grandchildren make their grand entrances into the world, seeing two of my daughters begin this incredible journey of motherhood, for all its ear-splitting, hair-pulling, heart-wrenching, giggle-making, sleep-depriving moments of wonder and miracles and pain and fear, and loving so furiously and intensely that you can hardly stand it.

I remember receiving the shattering news that changed everything, the horrible shock that meant I would be stuck on the other side of the planet away from all of them for long periods, when that was never in my plan on moving so far away.

I accept that this is how it must be - for now. But that does not lessen the pain of these years of separation, knowing I'm missing millions of moments of their lives, moments I can never get back, moments that are lost forever.

Every morning, I wake up in England and they are all in Calgary, thousands of miles away in Western Canada. Every morning, it is like tearing open a gaping wound in my heart and my soul, and I work to stitch it up so I can get through my days. It is a wound that never heals.

And twice a year, I'm slammed with Mother's Day, which always shreds that wound just a little bit more. My greatest joy has come from being a mother, and ironically it is also the source of my greatest pain because thousands of miles and an ocean separate me from my five children and five grandchildren, with no end to this in sight. Yes, I have the verdict on Mother's Day. Definitely more bitter than sweet. At least while I'm missing the lives of my children and grandchildren, one tick of the clock after another.

The only thing that connects us is love. Thank God for that.

60. Finding your voice in the midst of change.

Recently, a special friend wrote and told me that she's finding going into her 'middle years' harder than being a teen. She said she felt awkward; her voice isn't readily available to her; she wonders if this is a phase. Although it's only my humble opinion, I'm certain that she's right.

This is a time of change and discovery. It's more complicated than when we were teens because Life has been happening, we have been experiencing, we have gained many insights, taken hard knocks, loved as fiercely as we've hurt, and we are more complicated than when we were teens.

It was easy to find the voice of rebellion and inexperience. It is not so easy to sort through all that Life and Learning, and physical changes only add to the confusion.

The comments of this gentle soul came on the heels of a conversation I was having with someone else recently about the weird things my body is doing these days - and has been for some time. As it's aging and changing, and I'm in the throes of a particular set of 'changes' with heaven-knows-what ridiculous and seemingly unrelated symptoms popping up, I don't know what to expect any more. I mean, what the heck have ringing ears got to do with it? Or burning tongue? Or electric shocks? Dizziness?

I'd have thought absolutely nothing. But I'd have thought wrong.

Women's bodies change quietly from day to day with the subtlety of a feather knocking at the door. Not everyone pays close enough attention to notice those rhythmic changes, but I was always very much 'in tune' with my body.

But now, it's got a mind of its own. Problem is, it's got my mind, too.

I hear that problems with memory and concentration are also a part of this Mid-Life Misery that I'm supposed to embrace as a part of being a woman.

I've always been known for my exceptional memory, and while it's still far better than most, it's not the memory I'd come to expect throughout my life.

And now, my ability to concentrate is laughable. Years ago, I did 16 months' worth of a 4-year homeopathy program in 31 days - receiving an "A" for every one of the assignments.

But now?? Good grief, I love the English mists but I didn't really want a thick shroud of it inside my head. I know there's stuff in there I'm supposed to do, to remember, but it just disappears into the soup that I have to call my brain.

With my body having a mind of its own, while I hadn't got one at all any more, I was feeling a lot like my body had betrayed me. I felt lost. I didn't know what to expect any more - physically, mentally or emotionally. I didn't know what new symptoms might pop up and when, or whether they would be permanent fixtures in my life. There have been other changes, too, for other reasons, but they've all been happening simultaneously.

Of course I struggled to find my voice. It was because I struggled to find anything remotely resembling the woman I'd come to know so intimately for decades.

But then I realised that moving into these 'middle years' is just like moving house. You're not quite sure how you got there, but you look around and the house is different.

There are boxes everywhere. All this stuff you've accumulated in your life is there, jammed into those boxes. All that stuff is just waiting to find a home on a new shelf, or in a new little grouping with other goodies on a table or a wall.

Those boxes are filled with your experiences, all your pain, all your love and life and learning and happiness and hopes and wisdom and fear and healing - and all the words that go with them.

Whether you are changing because of age or circumstance or environment or trauma or money or for any other reason, sometimes it can be hard to find yourself or your voice. Especially when the changes are not within your control. We flow from one moment to the next, one experience to the next, and only once in a while lift our heads, look around and see that we're somewhere else. The river carried us away from Familiar and into Unknown.

But we've brought all our boxes with us. We just need to unpack them and all those words from all that 'stuff' will take a look around and find themselves lining up in new ways. They'll fit together in a different order; they'll define new spaces. And you'll get used to how all your stuff looks in your new home.

Rather than seeing change as a betrayal of everything familiar and safe, see it as a de-cluttering and reordering of what's important. See it as an opportunity to re-evaluate, to take stock, to reorganise your life, yourself, accepting it as just another step on your path to self-fulfillment.

Don't mind a little laryngitis along the way. Even a voice needs some rest and recovery now and then. You'll sing again, better, stronger and clearer than ever before.

61. Laughter is the best medicine.

Recently, I went to a beginner's stand-up comedy competition. I wanted to see what I'm in for when I give it a shot in a couple of months. Would the comedians be pelted with rotten fruit? Would the hecklers reduce them to tears or bring them to their knees?

Well, I'm happy to say that there was no rotten fruit, there were no tears, and the only guy who was on his knees did it as a part of his routine.

I don't know why it didn't occur to me before to see if I could find any comedy clubs near me. I've had such an isolated life since moving to England, it's ridiculous. Stuffed away in this cottage in a tiny village in the middle of nowhere, I've struggled to make friends - although thankfully, there have been a few - and I have found it just this side of impossible to have a social life.

Without my children and grandchildren around, there's been much less reason to laugh and be silly on a regular basis. To a large extent, humour had quietly disappeared from my life without so much as a whimper.

I've really missed the large doses of silliness and fun that used to permeate my life. Even when things were really difficult - and downright horrible many times - I still sought solace in jokes and used my sense of humour to get me through.

To be honest, there were also times when I sank so low with depression, that nothing made me laugh. Not even my favourite funny people or sit-coms. It took a crazy amount of stress and awful circumstances to land me there, but when I did, it was dark and empty. The light had gone out of my life entirely, and it was a really nasty place to be.

My recent decision to try my hand at stand-up has had me carrying a notebook around for weeks, filling page after page with one-liners, brief sketches, and a ridiculously long and growing list of topics which would be great for comedy writing. With the insane life I've led, man, have I got material...

I've been having loads of fun thinking about funny things, or thinking about things in a funny way, and I had a fantastic time at the club. I haven't laughed that much in ages; it was such a relief and did my heart (and even more so, my soul) a world of good.

Have you laughed today? Have you laughed recently? Are there funny people in your life? Do you enjoy reading or hearing good jokes? Do you watch "Live At The Apollo" or similar shows?

I hope you have lots of humour in your life, or if you don't, I hope you find it. You can sign up for a joke of the day to be emailed to you from various websites, or you can spend hours poring over funny stuff on the internet, especially on youtube, with loads of hilarious videos.

There are joke books, these comedy clubs, there are children - who are just naturally funny and they have no idea... wherever you can, reconnect with your sense of humour. Think back on events in your life that you thought were funny. Or perhaps you can find some that weren't so funny then, but they make you smile now.

They say laughter is the best medicine. Well, to be honest, I think it shares first place along with love and cuddles and feeling supported when life is kicking you in the head.

The good news is you don't even have to be sick to get a good dose of comedy or laughter. And you don't have to look very far to find it either.

Go on. Have a laugh. Have a bunch. They're pretty splendiferous. They make a bumpy life a lot better, and even if things are great for you, they'll be even better with a bit of comedy thrown in the mix.

And if you wanna make someone else's day lighter, share a joke or a funny story and enjoy the giggles.

62. Go for it now. Tomorrow is not a sure thing.

Got a dream? Got a wish? Got a little something you've always wanted to do but haven't because you didn't have the money or didn't have the time or blah blah blah fill in the blank with some excuse or other?

There may be a million reasons – and probably even more excuses – why you'd tell me you "can't" have or do what you want. And I'll concede that there are probably times that that's absolutely correct. Perhaps you've always wanted flying lessons but you're on benefits and struggling to afford food so all right, flying lessons are out for now because they're insanely expensive.

But what I'm getting at is that we can give up on our dreams too easily. Sometimes we don't even allow ourselves to consider whether or not we could make them happen. We dismiss them with "I could never do that" or "It would never work" or "I don't have the money."

And my favourite: "I don't have time."

That's actually the best reason to be pursuing your dream or your wish! You're right; you don't have time. The only time you have is this moment, right here, right now. There is no guarantee that there will be any other moments in the future. You don't have any time... to waste.

The point I'm trying to make is this: If there is something you would love to do, it's worth considering how you could make it happen. It's worth finding out what all the options are, asking questions, doing some investigating to see if you can overcome the obstacles. Even if you can't have it the way you want it right now, perhaps you can bring it into your life in some way.

So if you're on benefits and wanting those flying lessons, perhaps you could hang out at a flight school, ask if they need volunteer assistance. Maybe you'd at least learn some cool stuff and get the odd free spin through the clouds. That may not get you a pilot's license but you'd have a lot of fun and make friends who share your passion for flying.

Or maybe you'd always wanted to take a class in something but can't afford it or can't find one near you. Well, how about checking out youtube for instructions? There are lessons in all kinds of stuff! There's a wealth of information available on how to read Tarot, how to paint, how to do encaustic art, how to build things – there's loads of free instruction right there on the internet.

And there are loads of inexpensive instructional DVDs, too, for dance, exercise, martial arts, yoga – you don't have to leave home or spend lots of money to get fit or do things you enjoy.

Nothing's perfect. But getting to do something toward fulfilling your dreams is sure better than doing nothing.

Whatever it is that you want to add to your life, or change about it, is entirely up to you. Any restrictions are in your head, and that includes the long list of expectations or beliefs that other people have placed on what you do with your life. Those expectations create a prison in your head, and you're the only one who can keep yourself in it - or get yourself out of it.

Do you want to live out the rest of your days in that prison? Or do you want at least a little taste of freedom?

You are both the prisoner and the warden. You're the only one with the key. It's up to you to decide whether or not to use it.

63. Playtime Report!

Okay, kids. It's play time! What have you been doing to appease the little kid in you that is screaming for some attention?

Yesterday, I had a strawberry tart (with lots of whipped cream) and a bit of a chocolate bar with caramel in it for dinner.

And I've had lots more of that chocolate/caramel bar for parts of meals...or snacks in between!

Yesterday morning I had a two-hour nap. Yum. And I've had lots of other naps in the past couple of weeks. Lots and lots. Huge yum.

I spent extra time in an extra full tub with extra yummy-smelling bath salts yesterday afternoon. And it's a very, very big, deep tub so oooo boy, it was extra fab.

I've spent an hour a day doing Tai Chi for the past week.

And I've got back to meditating twice a day for a while now. How deliciously peaceful! What a difference it makes to the rest of my day.

I spent a whole bunch of time doodling recently. Very much fun, indeed!

I accepted a challenge to do stand-up and have been having a ton of fun writing material for my first competition. And I went to see how the competitions work by attending one recently and eegads, it was great fun!

I'd always wanted to learn belly dancing, so I'm rattling that coin belt now. And as I love lots of other dancing, I'm going to a funky smooth jive night (I think that's what it's called!) this week! Yippee!

I had ice cream for breakfast one day last week. The all-natural kind (that's the only kind I can stand!). Strawberry. Big yum.

I've ignored my laptop a lot and have made a conscious decision to spend way less time working and a bunch more time playing. Every day.

I spent the better part of a week in my jams doing whatever I darned well pleased – which was a whole lot of nothing but making like a slug. Truly fantastic. Loved every minute. Didn't give a rat's @$$ what the delivery guys and postman thought. They've seen me like that before. They'll see it again.

I've spent lots of time with the lights out in my room, staring at the pretty glass ball that rotates over gently bubbling water with several different colours changing and shining through it on my little desktop fountain. But it's not on my desk. It's on a little natural shelf in the exposed stone in my bedroom. It's right near my bed. I can lie there and watch the ball spin, see the beautiful colours changing every second or two, listen to the trickling water…and do absolutely nothing but enjoy every delicious moment. It's quite hypnotic, looking at that pretty little glass ball, nestled into the stone wall in the silence of my darkened room…

Recently, I've gone out with a friend or two; extra special treats!

I've gone to bed at ridiculously early times (for me) – like 10.30. Shocking. I'm usually just getting started by then and fighting with myself to go to bed at 3, 4, 5 a.m. But this little kid has been really sleepy lately so it's early bedtimes for her just now. How delightful!

I sat and watched a candle burning recently. Spent quite a while just watching the flame, and playing with the wax. It was very much fun! It's been years since I played with it, dripping it onto my skin and then peeling it off. Ya gotta know how to do it so you don't hurt yourself, though. Or ouch.

I've been feeding the kitty whose parents ignore her, and have been loving some of her very appreciative cuddles out on the patio. To heck with work. Kitty wants a cuddle. And so do I.

I indulged in a mani-pedi afternoon last week, hauled out the little tub of very hot water and all the bits and pieces, clippers, nail polish, a big fluffy soft towel etc. – and a glass of wine – plus, the remote control to get me through a bunch of recorded stuff.

And last night at my weekly gathering here at my home, I was launched into little kid-ness again (not that it takes much to launch me there. I kinda live there most of the time…) because I was given *the* coolest gift!!! Anyone who knows me very well (or anyone who was here for our yummy Tuesday evening group) is going to know how this next statement should sound (and for those of you who don't know, picture a 5-foot 9-inch 4-year-old with a lisp)…

I got purtiful new shooth!!!!! (pointing painted toenails show-offingly whilst admiring new sandals) And they're *thparkly!!!!!!!*

There was no part of me that could even pretend to act like a grown-up when Katie gave me those beautiful sandals last night. I squealed and giggled and danced around in my new shoes like a little kid. And kept squealing and giggling periodically throughout the evening when there was a lull in the conversation, and I'd say again, while pointing toes show-offingly, *"I got purtiful new shooth!!!!"*

Thank you for my purtiful NEW SHOOOOTH, Katie!! xxxxxxxxxxxxxx

So. What delicious bits of play time have you been up to?? And if you know there's a shortage, don'tcha think it's time to fix that?

C'mon…you know you wanna!!

:o)

64. Be open to how you can serve. Be a Miracle Worker.

I'll bet you've had at least one miracle in your life. And quite probably, a lot more. No doubt you were ever so grateful for each and every one of them.

It's possible that you need another one now. If so, I hope you get it. And in the meantime, you can *be* a miracle for someone else.

Sometimes it doesn't take much to make a monumental difference in someone's life, to give a bit of hope, a little relief, and to you, what you did might not be a big deal, but to them, it means the world.

There are people in need everywhere. They're in need of a visit, a lift to a medical appointment, or information about a support service. They need a meal made, a kitchen tidied, a load of laundry done. They need a little fresh air, a prescription collected, help with homework.

They might just need to know someone cares.

As you go about your life, rushing through one hectic day after another, diving into a full workload and being busybusybusy thinking about what you have to do and where you have to be, watch for ways to make a difference for someone else. It doesn't have to take more than a kind word, or just a few moments of your time to listen. You might hear people say they need something that you could manage to do.

And remember, people don't always say, "I need...." Sometimes you have to "listen between the lines". Or maybe even ask, "What do you need?"

If you keep yourself open to serving others, you will find plenty of opportunities, both big and small, to work miracles in the lives of others.

You may not even know you did it. But that's not the point. The point is, they'll have got their miracles. And you know how that feels when it's you.

65. **People are presents.**

Every person you meet is like an unwrapped present, even if it's a one-time meeting, even if you bristle, even if you don't see it at the time.

Everyone with whom you interact will reveal something about yourself, if you pay attention, and the gift of self-awareness allows you to be more fulfilled and ultimately live a happier life.

Some people may appear to touch you more than others. Something connects your soul and theirs in a way that is inexplicable. Familiar, certain, strong, frightening, wonderful, exciting; you don't need words but there is no denying what has happened.

But whether it is perceived as a positive meeting or a negative one, with just one reaction from you, you have inadvertently created a chain of events that ties you together, suspending that moment in your history forever. This is how powerful you are.

Even if you do nothing at all, you can connect with the energy of other people. You may simply walk down the street and it happens as you pass them, glance at them, or smile at them.

But that exchange, no matter how brief, gives both you and the other person an opportunity to learn something about yourselves. It may be strength, it may be fear, but seeing you can trigger something within them that could lead to a major transformation and you will never know anything about it.

And that works both ways.

No matter how weak you think you are, it is your power, and not your powerlessness, which is what can really frighten you. Once you understand and accept this, you have the key to tapping into your power and creating ripples and waves that benefit you and everyone you meet. It's like tapping into the energy of all other people, connecting everyone all together, and leading all of us in the direction of growth and fulfilment.

We are not separate from each other, but rather, we are particles of energy that collide and affect each piece of solid matter that they hit.

Your energy has the potential to affect everyone you walk past, everyone with whom you speak or interact, even briefly. In one way or another, you have the power to initiate great change and transformation in others, whether you know it or not.

Contemplate your energy, your power. Consider how it radiates, the message it gives. Then align it with your spirit and maximise the potential for it to serve its highest purpose.

66. To be able to ask for help is a blessing.

Early this morning, I was awakened by the sounds of some poor soul quite obviously in distress. I nodded off.

After a while, I was awakened once again, and the cries were more frequent. They increased in pitch, as the distress became more urgent.

I wondered what was wrong, wondered what was causing such desperation. But there was nothing I could do but be grateful that I wasn't the one in trouble.

Could I not have picked up the phone and dialed 999? Could I not have got up, got dressed, gone out to see if I could help?

No, on both counts, because the distress was coming from one of the cows across the lane. The farmer is there. He could hear it even better than I, and he knows his cow things so he would tend to it as he'd see fit.

Besides, I've not got a clue about broken cows. Kids, yes. Cows, no.

As I listened to this poor cow's increasing suffering, I thought about how lucky we are to be able to seek help when we need it. At least, those of us who don't live in Third World Countries, those of us who are privileged enough to have friends and family, telephones, doctors, hospitals, support groups, alternative health care options, emergency services, neighbours, even strangers who sometimes appear out of nowhere and make a huge difference in our times of need.

I thought about how lucky we are to be able to verbalise what's wrong. What hurts, what's missing, what's so urgent. We're so blessed to be able to speak up and get the help we need, yet so often, we don't. For many of us, it is difficult to say, "I need help." We don't want to be weak. We don't want to bother anyone. We're afraid of being dependent. We don't deserve it. The list goes on and on.

And I've been one of the worst for this. As a child, I learned very early that there was no help for the worst of my suffering. I was not protected in my home, and suffered at the hands of those who were meant to care for me. There was nowhere to go for help. It never even occurred to me to ask because I had been taught that I did not matter.

And I grew up not asking. I spent my adult life not asking. And even when it was offered, it was like amputating a limb without anaesthetic to say 'yes please'. Why? Well, a variety of reasons. I had been taught I didn't deserve anything good, I didn't deserve to be heard. I was not important. My feelings and needs did not matter. And I was flat out told repeatedly that I was not as good, as valued, or worth as much as other people.

So why would I think I deserved any help? Why would I think my needs mattered? Of course, I did not.

What is extra sad about this is that I know I am not alone. Far too many in the people have been treated the same way, leading to the same result.

This issue of not accepting or asking for help has been multi-faceted and has required many years of chipping away at its various aspects, healing several different issues that contributed to it. It's been one of the most difficult lessons of my life because it sits right on top of those core issues.

In recent years, I've got better at both asking for help and accepting it when it's offered, although it still feels like I'm wearing shoes that are two sizes too small when I do it. But at least I do it.

A couple of years ago, it occurred to me that I've been asking the universe for certain blessings. Pretty basic stuff, really. Being with my family, having the ability to support myself, and devoting my life to charity work in a very big way. I've needed a miracle or two to make all of this happen.

Suddenly, I realised that I'd been putting up a huge stumbling block and if I didn't remove it, I was never going to get my miracle. All my life, I'd been a "giver". But I wasn't very good at receiving.

And if I didn't know how to receive, why would the universe bother to give me what I wanted?

What was extra interesting is that as soon as I realised that I needed to learn how to receive, I was given some huge lessons in how to do it. There were massive offers from friends who wanted to help in ways I needed desperately. My first instinct was, as usual, to say "No, thank you."

But I did not.

I saw that the universe was trying to help me. It was saying, "Here you go! Lessons on learning how to receive! Hurry up, because we have Big Things to give you, if you'll just learn how to accept them!"

So I choked on "Yes, thank you." And many times since then, it's been stuck in my throat but I keep swallowing and eventually, it gets easier.

And the miracles have begun. I haven't got The Really Big One Yet, but several smaller ones have made their way into my life. The universe is responding to my willingness to ask for help, and to receive it gratefully when it is offered.

How blessed we are to be able to verbalise what we need and to manifest what our hearts desire. It is far too precious a gift to be wasted.

67. Another way to let your light shine

If I were to ask you if you're a creative person, what would you say? Some of you who are reading this will say "Yes"; some of you will say "No".

Of the ones who say "No", I'm gonna dispute that. I'm gonna say "Yes, you are." And you'll say, "No, I'm not. I haven't got a creative molecule in my body. I don't paint, I don't draw, I don't sculpt, I don't write books or music. I'm not creative. Full stop."

But, my friend, there are waaaaaaaaay more ways to be creative than just those. Of course there are the obvious ones. Sewing, knitting, crochet, needlework etc. There is also carpentry, cabinet-making and all sorts of woodworking. There's gardening, landscaping, interior design, architecture, painting, wallpapering, home decoration.

There's dancing, singing, telling jokes, baking, cooking, acting. In being a mechanic or having a 'knack' for taking things apart, fixing them, and putting them back together.

How you express yourself, what you do, what's important to you, who you are - these are some of the ways in which your creativity manifests. There is creativity is being very organised, and finding storage solutions with limited space. There's creativity in problem-solving, in time management, in public speaking.

There's creativity in having a brain that's good with numbers, in being playful, in teaching, in learning.

You are always creating, whether you think about it or not. You are always creating your world, your life. You create friendships, relationships, career path, new interests. Everything about your essence, as you move from one moment to the next, is creating something. Whether it's something wonderful or something painful, or something just for fun, you are always creating.

We are 'creatures' of habit - in other words, we 'create' our habits. And from those habits, we create our environments and our futures. Those habits are in our behaviour, what we do with our time, how we live our lives. They are the thoughts we think, over and over again. We can keep habits we like, we can break the ones we don't, and even in that, we are being creative - creating a new way of thinking, a new way of being. You are creating your life, one moment at a time.

The more you think about everything you do as being creative, the more you will see your creative nature, and the power you have to cultivate and create more in your life than you thought possible.

The more you think of yourself as a creative being, and allow yourself to explore your creativity, the more you will feel a sense of freedom and fulfillment in your life.

Expressing yourself through your creativity, whether it's in how you organise your paper clips and thumbtacks, or whether you paint magnificent works of art, is how you will get to know yourself in ways you never did before, and it will allow the rest of us to get to know the beauty that lies hidden deep inside you.

The more you open yourself up in this way, the more you let your light shine.

Take a little time today and think about all the ways in which you create your world and everything you put in it. I'm sure you'll be surprised by how many you discover, no matter how creative you already are.

68. **You are a duvet that cannot be put back in the bag.**

Do you feel stuck? Are you in limbo? Do you feel like you're always the same, day after day, and nothing changes?

Look at where you were a couple of years ago. For some of you, things might be very obviously different from how they were back then. For others of you, they might seem to be exactly the same.

On the surface, I could say that about my own situation. Two years ago, I was living in this cottage, doing generally what I'm doing now, still waiting for the Big Miracle that I mentioned recently. Yup, if I just look at the surface, I feel like I'm spinning my wheels.

But in truth, there have been many profound changes for me, both personally and professionally. I've taken enormous steps that have moved me a whole lot closer to that Big Miracle than I ever believed possible.

And I am a very, very different woman from who I was two years ago. Sure, some of the basics are still there. I'm compassionate, silly, emotional, sensitive, and very determined (some would say stubborn, but that's only when I'm not doing what they think I should be doing). I'm still just a 5'9" tall 4-year-old most of the time.

My plans and I still get together for our regular morning meeting, agree on what needs doing, but then go our separate ways. We like our independence, my plans and I.

Some things never change. But in countless ways, I have changed. The past two years have been extremely difficult; among the hardest I've ever endured. I've been forced to accept some very painful truths. I've been forced to do things I would never have done in the past. I've been forced to become a very different person.

What's this, you ask? Me, being forced? Am I not always on about how we have the freedom to choose, to be what we want, to think for ourselves? Do I not keep insisting that you can make your dreams come true?

How can I say all of that, and turn around and tell you I've been forced into all this pain and difficulty?

The truth is, I forced myself. And I did it because I knew it was right for me. Enormous obstacles had been thrown in my path. Monumental, heartbreaking obstacles that tore at me like I cannot begin to describe. The writing was on the wall, but I refused to accept it until I ended up with a life-threatening health crisis.

I dreaded even contemplating those obstacles. If not for that health crisis, it would have been so much easier to turn back, to avoid them. To pretend they did not exist. I could have taken the easy way out and stayed where I was, not made the changes that were thrown in my path.

Yes, I could have done that.

But I knew that I would have been completely and utterly miserable. I knew I would have been deliberately turning my back on my destiny, my potential, my spirit. And I knew that my health crisis was a direct result of living in a situation that despite the good parts was extremely destructive to me on all levels, as much as I did not want to believe it.

There have been many times along the way that I've wished I could turn back. So many times I've agonised over what I know now, but wish I did not. So many painful tears burning down my face like branding irons, my heart aching to push away changes and realities I couldn't bear to accept.

But have you ever taken a new duvet out of the plastic bag in which it arrived? You just can't imagine how they stuffed that whole thing in there because it comes billowing out like a mountain of foam. And then you try to get it all back in the bag. It can't be done.

I was the duvet. My knowledge had expanded. I had expanded. I could see things I hadn't seen before. I had new awarenesses, new strengths, new learning, and as heartbreaking as it was, there was no way I could align them with who I used to be. Somewhere along the way, I had become someone else. I had found myself on a completely different path from the one I thought I'd always been on throughout my entire life. And I hadn't even seen it coming.

I needed to be on this path; it's where I'm meant to be. I have no choice.

Not if I'm going to be happy. Not if I'm going to fulfill what I believe is my destiny.

Two years ago, I began a massive transformation and rebirth. Now, it's like I have been given a second life - quite literally. If you only knew just what I mean...but that is a whole other story.

I'm grateful for all of the changes in myself on a personal level; they needed to happen.

And I'm grateful for where I am now, and although I have hopes and ideas about where I'm headed, I shall just have to wait and see what the universe has in store for me. I trust in its wisdom, knowing that it always gives us what we need, even if it's not always what we want.

When I was young, my two best childhood friends were killed in an accident. Many years later, their mother had some words of wisdom for me. She said, "You never get over the pain. You just learn to live with it."

Some things are just like that. As for the painful, difficult bits I left behind with the 'old me', I carry that pain with me every single day. But it's okay because it reminds me of some of the greatest love and the greatest joy I've ever known, and to which I had to say goodbye.

You may not notice the changes in yourself or your life. But you have had experiences, conversations, events that will have contributed to your evolution. You can never go back to who you used to be. You are that billowing duvet, whether you can see it or not.

This is a good thing. It means you're moving forward in your life. And it's the only direction worth travelling.

69. For the love of nourishment

For those of you who are regular readers here, you'll know about the little kitty whose parents have chucked her out and left her to fend for herself. She is the most affectionate, purring loving little ball of fur, just aching to be cuddled and she's ever so grateful for every scratch and stroke, every bit of food I give her.

This morning, I went down to the porch, where I keep her food and water, and a little box with a towel in it, so she has a warm little bed when it's cold and wet outside. Thank heaven for cat flaps, and the fact that there was already one in the door when I moved to this cottage several years ago.

She was waiting patiently for me and began meowing like mad as I opened the little pouch of prawns in jelly. She devoured her food hungrily, almost as fast as I could squeeze it out onto a plate, purring loudly in between gulps. I couldn't help but remember those times I saw her in my rubbish bins outside, or eating chicken bones she'd pulled out onto the drive.

Knowing she belonged to someone in the village, I thought she was just having a little snack at those times, until she wandered into the garden one day when I was out on the patio and I saw how frighteningly bony she had become since she used to come and visit. I realised she was not being fed at all any more.

After making sure she was fed, I went to the fridge in search of my own breakfast. It's filled with cheeses, fresh vegetables, eggs, a yummy soup I made a couple of days ago, and more.

The cupboards are also filled with biscuits and pasta, rice and snacks, tins of beans, jars of pickles and sauces, and all sorts of other goodies.

Every time I eat something, I am grateful for it. I'm grateful for the fact that

I live in a part of the world where there is an abundance of food, and that I was not born into a country where there is none.

And every day I am ashamed to live in a part of the world where so much food is wasted, when every moment that I am eating, in fact every moment that I am breathing, there are people wasting away and starving to death. Mothers holding their skeleton children, too weak to move, too weak to cry, until they draw one last breath and slip away to a place where there is no more suffering.

I don't ever forget those people and I sit in tears while watching the adverts that plead for £2 a month to help feed them. I give them as much as I can but of course it's a drop in the bucket.

And of course, there are plenty of people in our parts of the world who do not have enough to eat. It is a crime that if you live in an affluent country, there is no guarantee that everyone will be fed, or have a home, or access to good medical care.

It is late spring. The end of May. People are contemplating holidays, warmer weather coming, barbecues, picnics, days at the beach. It's not mid-November, early December, when that Christmas spirit hits and people start remembering those who have no jobs, no homes, no food, and they decide it's time to do their bit, get involved, give to a charity, work at a soup kitchen for a few hours, feed the homeless.

When you've got food in your fridge and in your cupboards, even if it's not a lot and it's simple fare, it's so easy not to think about the horrors of hunger, and what it must be like to go without food.

There are people in the world, both near and far, who need your help. There are people who need food, who wake up sick with hunger every morning, and go to bed the same way every night.

There are people who have to watch their children go hungry, who feel the shame, the heartache, the trauma of hearing their cries, knowing they're desperate for food, and some of them are right here, down your street, across the lane, in your village, at your children's school.

We can forget their hunger. We can ignore it. But they cannot. They do not have that privilege.

Can you give £2 a month to a charity? Or $2? Or a couple of tins of food to the nearest food bank? Can you ask at the schools or churches if there's a family in need and see if you can help with a meal now and then, or perhaps a bag of groceries? Can you give that university student or struggling young waitress, who is away from family and living on beans on toast, a proper meal?

Can you help to get the world just a little nearer to a place of balance, a place where everyone is properly nourished and no one has to worry about when - or whether - they will eat again?

Of course you can. But will you?

70. If you're struggling to get to 'happy', you can at least intend 'relief'.

Your feelings are a direct result of your thoughts. If you're feeling good, you're having good thoughts. If you're feeling bad, you're thinking about stuff that makes you feel bad.

When you change your thoughts, you change your feelings. Yeah, I know, it isn't easy. But does it have to be? Just because something is difficult or takes practice before it gets easier, does that mean you shouldn't do it?

In the words of the fictitious Al Borland on the hit TV show, *Home Improvement*, "I don't think so, Tim."

You are in control of your thoughts. You get to be in charge of what goes through your head. Sure, some stuff wanders in there unbidden. And some of that is not happy stuff. So tell it to get out. Send it packing and replace it with thoughts that make you feel good.

When another unhappy thought wanders through again, send it packing, too, and keep filling your head with positive thoughts.

Okay, when you're feeling really miserable, it can be quite a stretch to think about happy stuff. So try this: Focus on relief. If it's too much for you to have the intention to be happy, then intend to feel relief. Just keep telling yourself that you intend to feel relief, you are feeling relief... anything that gets you thinking about relief. Try words like peace, calm, soothing.

Then imagine how it will feel to be relieved. Close your eyes, *feel* the relief. Just hold that vision, hold that feeling...

The more you take yourself out of your miserable thoughts and allow yourself to have relief thoughts or happy thoughts, the quicker you will be out of the misery and into feeling better.

I know that when jobs are lost and money is tight and debts are high and health is poorer than you are, it seems ridiculous to imagine being happy - or feeling relief. So you look for the blessings, look for the good bits, look for what works, and get a little balance for the gloom and doom.

You can at least intend to have relief. And you can intend that as many times a day as you want and it will make a difference - if you let it.

71. A bit of Karma for the mini-Hitlers in our midst

I refuse to read newspapers, watch news on TV or listen to it on the radio. I figure if there's anything I really need to know, people will tell me. I can't stand to hear about the suffering in the world.

It's bad enough when it's an "Act of God" or some terrible accident. But I simply cannot tolerate hearing about the dreadful things people do to each other. There are few things in the world that are worse than when one human being causes *any* kind of suffering to another.

There is no need for that at all. It is beneath our dignity. It goes completely against the divine spirit that resides in everyone. It is human behaviour at its worst, and spiritual behaviour at its most absent.

What springs to mind are the usual kinds of suffering that are always in the news - beatings, rape, kidnapping, torture, murder and so on.

But there is a much more insidious and far less visible kind of suffering than these very obvious ones. There is the emotional suffering that is caused by gossip, vindictiveness, or jealousy. There is the torment that is caused by vicious and judgemental attacks against others, or by telling people horrible things about someone else in an effort to turn others against that person.

I am outraged every time I hear about people who choose to believe vicious and vindictive talk about someone else without having any personal knowledge or experience of such incidents. That 'sheep mentality' is what gets us into so much trouble; it is how Hitler became such a hit in the eyes of his followers. They followed the herd. They believed the rubbish that was crammed down their throats by fear-based, power-hungry, hateful bullies.

I am even more outraged every time I hear about the people who have launched just such a campaign of hatred, and who do their level best to get a group of people on their side against others, so they can gang up on them, bully them, verbally assault them, tell everyone horrible things to make them hate those people.

For some small-minded "reason", there are those who choose to be vindictive and nasty in their attempts to scapegoat others. It is disgusting. It is shocking. It is appalling.

What's worse is that if you ask these people why they spread their hateful talk the way they do, they'll tell you that they're justified. They use their own opinions (justified or not) as weapons. They act as though they have the right to trash another person to anyone who will listen. They defend their actions as if they're the actions of the pure and innocent, when in fact, they come from mean-spirited, vengeful, vindictive, fearful, power-hungry, judgemental hearts and they could stand to take a good, long look in the mirror.

Whatever they think is so awful about so-and-so that they should be spreading their hateful and vindictive comments and opinions so freely can't possibly be anywhere near as bad as their deliberate and vicious verbal assaults on another human being, whether directly or indirectly aimed at that person.

What further offends me is when such people are two-faced, or when they pretend to be very spiritual and loving in other arenas or with other people - and if it weren't so twisted it would almost be hilarious but sometimes they even say they are healers!!! - then they turn around and treat others in a way that is downright evil because it is deliberate. Their desire is to hurt, to attack, to be judgemental, to make one person hate or avoid another.

Very young children can be excused from such behaviour because they're usually all playing together again in five minutes anyway. There is *no excuse* for such reprehensible behaviour in adults who understand the social and emotional ramifications of it. What makes it even more disgusting is that it is precisely because of those ramifications that they do it. They want that person to suffer. They want that person to be hated by others. How malignant, how destructive, how evil...

Thank heaven for the Law of Karma. The universe does not judge. It has no consciousness. It just balances positive and negative energy, and if you put loads of negative energy out there, you're going to get it back at some point. For every action, there is an equal and opposite reaction. Throw a ball straight ahead of you at a wall, it will bounce right back and slam you in the face.

One way or another, what we do will eventually come back to us. Those who launch verbal assaults on others, whether directly to those people, or indirectly by spreading vicious attacks on someone's character to someone else, might do well to remember this.

72. Two wrongs don't make a right.

Yesterday, I said that the Law of Karma is like throwing a ball at a wall in front of you, and having it bounce back and hit you in the face.

Whatever you put out, you will get back. It's a promise. The universe balances negative and positive energy all the time. That's what karma is. Guaranteed, you'll get yours - whether it's good - or not.

It's good to remember this: What other people do affects their karma. What you do in response affects yours.

If you hear someone else's negative viewpoint of someone, do you take it as truth? Do you take it on as your own opinion? Do you then choose to look at that person with disdain - whether or not you know that person yourself?

Do you speak about a person negatively to others? Do you spread gossip and rumours, or share your low opinion of that person with other people?

Do you treat that person as if they have the plague? Do you make judgements without ever having met them or having first-hand knowledge of anything untoward?

Look at the relationships in your life - and by that, I mean the people with whom you interact in any way. Are there people who are negative, vindictive, or just plain toxic? How does it feel to be around those people?

Chances are, you don't like it very much. If you can take steps to avoid or ignore them, it's best for your health (and theirs; we don't want you to slam them upside the head with a two-by-four...!)

So if you don't like being around people like that, be sure that you don't become one of them. If you want people to see you as kind and loving, then be that way. If you want them to think of you as a spiritual, positive influence, then be that way.

If you want people to tell others that you're compassionate and caring, then be that way. If you want to hear people say you do many thoughtful and generous things, then be that way.

It's not enough to exhibit all of these wonderful qualities when it's convenient and then open your mouth and say hurtful things about others - even if you think you're right. Whether or not you are is irrelevant. It is unfair and damaging, and it doesn't make you look good in the eyes of others either.

If you don't like the fact that other people say hurtful things about you, then stop similar words from falling out of your own mouth about them.

Retaliation only makes matters worse. Like they say, two wrongs do **not** make a right. They just add loads of fuel to an already-roaring fire.

At all times, strive to be the person you want people to think you are and let the universe take care of karma. Keep your own nose clean and never mind anyone else's. They'll get their just reward someday. And so will you.

Before you open your mouth and spread dirt about someone, whether or not you think you're justified, whether or not you believe you have a valid reason, remember to throw sweet flower petals at that wall, rather than a big, hard ball, because whatever you chuck at it, it's gonna come back some day. You will be given a mirror for your own actions.

So choose them wisely.

73. There's your side, their side, and the truth.

Millions of bits of information and experience are logged in our brains and in our souls. The accumulation begins when we're still warm and snug inside our mothers' bodies. Adrenalin crosses the placenta, so when Mummy feels stressed and anxious, so does her baby. Although muted, we hear her angry or fearful voice, and those of anyone with whom she is arguing. We can also hear soothing sounds of love and feel the chemical changes in her body when she is relaxed and at peace.

We are born and immediately begin experiencing life in another way. Our environments teach us what to expect - even if it is the unexpected, the unpredictable.

By the time we reach adulthood, we've had a wealth of experience that acts like a filter through which we view everything that happens to us or around us. It colours everything we think, feel, hear and see.

When I was studying homeopathy, the class would sometimes witness a case-taking. We would all be present at the same time, hearing the same patient give the same information, giving the practitioner mental, emotional and physical symptoms in detail.

We would then work out the case as we'd been taught, choosing which particular bits of information we thought were essential in determining which remedy to give.

It was always surprising to me how a room full of people could look at the same patient at the same time and come up with so many different aspects to a case at once, and with several different remedies offered up as possibilities - when the trick is to find the one that is correct. But this is because of our filters.

For example: A little girl loves her daddy. They're very close. They spend lots of time playing together. He takes her to the park, reads stories, plays games. Sometimes he puts her in the car for a special day out, just the two of them. She grows up and sees other daddies with their little girls and thinks how lovely it is. She thinks the little girls are very lucky.

Another little girl fears her daddy. He is too close. He spends lots of time doing very bad things to her. Sometimes he puts her in the car and takes her to a place where no one can see what they are doing, just the two of them. She grows up and sees the same daddies with the same little girls as the other woman saw, and she thinks how terrifying it is. She thinks the little girls are very much abused.

These very different filters colour the same situation in two very different ways.

When we have problems with other people, a disagreement, some sort of altercation, our filters give us our perception of what happened. Whatever we think about it is what makes us feel the way we do.

It is the same for those who are on the other side of it. Their filters will give them a viewpoint that comes from their own experiences and beliefs. Unrelated past emotional wounds can twist and distort reality, although it is not necessarily obvious. Personality clashes also play a part in creating differing perspectives on the same situation.

So there's your side, and there's their side. And somewhere outside both experiences of the same event lies the truth. Somewhere in the mess that has been created are the facts, plain and simple, the unvarnished truth of the matter. No emotions involved, no history, just facts - exactly what was said and done, as it unfolded, without any judgement, as seen by the eyes of the universe. How all parties view the situation, and what they choose to do with it, is often quite another story.

Sometimes we try to cram 'our side' down the throats of others. We want to be heard. We need to be believed. We want to be right.

But at what cost? At the cost of our dignity? Our self-respect? And what about the cost to innocent bystanders? To people who get caught in the crossfire? What about the damage done to them?

Understanding that others do not necessarily share your viewpoint doesn't make it any less valid. And it doesn't necessarily make theirs any less valid either. But when we can accept that all of us are human, all of us make mistakes, all of us get things wrong, all of us are flawed, and every one of us has a filter that never quits, perhaps this can help to settle differences. Perhaps we can simply agree to disagree and get on with our lives, and if there are innocent bystanders who were damaged in the wreckage, perhaps an apology is in order, followed by doing anything possible to leave them out of it in the future.

There comes a time for peace. For healing. Our world and so many people in it could use a good dose of both. Perhaps today, and every day, there's something you can do about that.

74. You can't heal till you know what needs healing.

Recently, I've been having a little physical issue. In watching it unfold, I can't help but see how the healing process is the same as it is for emotional wounds. It's been an interesting reminder about how we have the ability to go from pain to wellness - although sometimes things have to get a little worse before they get a lot better.

A couple of weeks ago, I had a biopsy. A little chunk was taken out of my inner ankle, not a nice place for the sting of needles with that nasty burning anaesthetic. But at least it wasn't quite as horrible as having several of them in the arch of my foot some years back, for the removal of a mole that was trying to be melanoma when it grew up.

So anyway, the doc took out this little chunk of my foot and stitched the hole together. I was told not to remove the dressing for a week. But I've had a few such procedures in my life, and on the fourth day, I knew this was just *not* feeling right. It was hurting way too much. It didn't help that it was in a place that moved with even the slightest movement of my foot so it was constantly being irritated.

I removed the dressing and discovered that all the stitches had come out - well, there were two left at one end but they weren't holding anything together any more. They'd come apart but were still stuck in my skin, and there was a gaping hole where a little piece of me used to be.

Actually, it looked kinda cool. Sorta like a bullet hole, I'm guessing, remembering my shooting days and what my guns did to the targets, only this was in technicolour.

The district nurse came round, took a look, redressed it and said to leave it till I saw the doc a few days later. As I feared would happen, by the time I got there, the wound had begun to heal with the stitches in it. So it had to be ripped open to get them out.

If I thought it had been hurting the previous week, I was wrong. Eegads. I had to stay 'stop' at one point; the pain was so intense, it was making me quite sick. But finally, the last stitches were out.

For the next few days, it was more painful than at any time since having the procedure. The entire area around my ankle and heel has been swollen, purple, red, and has caused me a fair bit of grief, even when I'm not shuffling through the cottage rather gingerly.

In the midst of this going on, recently I was doing some counselling work with someone. During the session, my client divulged some extremely painful experiences from her younger years. She has dreaded thinking about them, and the idea of speaking about them was even worse.

However, through our session, she could see that she's been dragging these issues around with her since they happened. She could see that they've been affecting her feelings of self-worth and self-esteem. She sees that they've affected her relationships and that ignoring those wounds isn't the same as healing them.

She and I are going to have to do a little digging. Her own repair attempts have done as much good as my stitches that had come apart. There has been a gaping wound in her soul, but the emotional damage that was done for years has been there, stuck in the middle of any efforts to heal.

Just as my wound was trying to heal around those stitches, this woman's wounds would never heal properly under the dressing of her silence. They would continue to fester, cause infection, create one problem after another in her life.

I know what this is like. I carried the memories and scars of all kinds of abuse for many years. It's horrible to live with it; it's terrifying to look at it. But what sweet relief when you make it past that point and into a place of strength and healing...

When we experience a painful or traumatic emotional event, it changes us. Even if we shove it to the side and try to pretend it doesn't exist, it's just like the hole that was closing up around those useless stitches and hiding under the dressing on my foot. It doesn't just go away because we don't talk about it. It doesn't just go away because it happened a long time ago and we don't think about it much any more. It's all still there, just like those damned stitches in my wound as it tried to close around them.

There comes a time when we must be brave and face what hurts us. We must bring it out into the light where we can see it, and actively do something about it. This is how we become stronger. We stop letting our pain control our lives, because if we don't, we're giving our power to the people who caused the damage in the first place, and we're allowing them to ruin the future.

Today the swelling and discolouration are still there but finally, for the first time, I've noticed an actual decrease in the pain. Although I'm far from dancing a little jig, I can tell I've turned a corner and this thing is finally healing.

Take heart, if you are suffering. This is just a little reminder that we are capable of great healing - on all levels. The first step is to uncover andaddress what it is that needs to be healed.

And that step is also the first on your road to peace and happiness.

75. If the mountain won't come to Mohammed...

I have a very dear friend who really detests cloudy, cool, rainy weather (you know who you are!). She loves, needs, craves fresh air, the outdoors, going for walks, and feels very confined, restricted and "suffocated" when she's forced to remain inside because it's not a nice, sunny day. Most people watch talk shows, sit-coms, and "regular TV". But not this friend of mine. Nope. She watches the weather channel!

In all my life, I don't believe I've ever met anyone else who does that. I mean, apart from wanting a quick weather-check to see what clothing you need for the day or whether you should still go ahead with those picnic plans.

No, my friend turns it on and watches. And watches. And watches. And watches! It's something I've always found to be rather weird but very endearing about her at the same time. But hey, it's me, so I can do weird, no problem. That's probably why it's also endearing!

Another thing about my sweet friend, she's always drinking water. My goodness, I thought I was bad for that but she probably consumes half of Niagara Falls in any given day. Always a bottle or a glass of the clear stuff

being lifted to her mouth. I'm sure she hooks herself up to one of those hamster bottles at night so she can keep sipping while she sleeps!

She goes on and on at length about loving blooming flowers and leaves coming out on trees. Adores nature at the height of its summertime glory. She spent some time here with me a while ago and was extremely excited by the fact that we have colourful flowers and greenery everywhere; then she went back home where there wasn't one leaf to be seen and not a splash of colour anywhere.

Recently, she wrote to say one or two things were just beginning to grow again and she was like a little kid, so excited about spring finally making its tentative appearance.

Then just a couple of days ago, she wrote to tell me the weather was enough to make her hop off a cliff! "SOOOOOO much rain", she said.

If I ever want to know what mood she's in, all I have to do is check the weather where she lives. That's all the information I need. No point in even writing to ask!

I don't like it when my friends are in distress. So after years of listening to her being in such a knot about wet weather, I figured perhaps I'd stop being sympathetic, as that wasn't at all useful, and try to offer some assistance. So after receiving her email about her weather woes the other day, I got on the horn.

"Do you remember how much you loved loved loved the flowers and greenery when you were here?"

"Oh, yes!!!!! It was SO BEAUTIFUL!"

"Do you remember how much you hated going back home and finding not even one little leaf waiting to greet you?"

"Oh, yeah, that was awful! It was so brown and dead! It just looked --"

I interrupted. I knew where she was headed! "And you really hate the rain!"

"Yes! It makes me feel so miserable! I can't get out for any air!" (Yes, darling, I know... and I understand!)

"Well, if you want the pretty flowers and all that green stuff, you have to put up with the rain, right?"

A brief silence. The wheels began to turn. A hesitant. "Ye-e-e-es."

"And have you noticed how thirsty you are and how much water you need, and how much of it you're always drinking?"

More silence. A few grinding gears, and then "Ye-e-e-es."

"Well, where do you think it comes from? You love to water your garden. You need to drink lots of water. What happens when it doesn't rain for a long time? We have droughts. Stuff dies. Our consumption of water is restricted. If it goes on long enough, we die, too. Don't you think it's time you started to love the rain?"

"Oh! I never looked at it that way before!"

"Be grateful for the rain! Thank the rain! Appreciate the rain! You have no control over the rain. You have no control over the fact that gardens need it, the earth needs it, we need it - everyone and everything will die without it. You cannot change any of that.

"So if you have a problem with rain but you can't change it. The only thing you can do to feel better about it is so change how you view the rain."

A big, bright halogen moment hovered over her head as she understood what I was saying. She was very excited about this new perspective and thought perhaps it would help her cope with rainy weather in the future. I hope it does because I don't like it when she's feeling miserable.

When you cannot change a situation that distresses, irritates or annoys you in any way, the only thing you can do to feel better is to change how you view it. A shift in your perspective can go a lo-o-o-o-o-o-ong way to making you much happier.

76. Don't think about a green striped apple.

Don't think about a green striped apple. Whatever else you think about for the next two minutes, do not think about a green striped apple.

Think about rainbows or flowers or cats in pyjamas or a new house or marshmallows but just don't think about a green striped apple. Don't imagine what it looks like, don't imagine what kind of green it is, don't imagine whether the stripes are vertical, horizontal, or twisty ones like a barber pole (oh, that would be pretty if it was spinning!). Don't wonder if it's a red apple with alternating green stripes, or if it's an apple that is only different colours of green stripes. Get any images of a green striped apple out of your head.

On another topic... What have you done so far today? Depending on where you are in the world, and what time zone you're in, and what time you read this, that might only be that you've barely got out of bed. Or you could be heading back there shortly.

Was it a good day - or is it shaping up that way? What have you got on your mind right now? Work stuff? Deadlines? Laundry? Playtime? If that green striped apple wanders through, don't think about it!

Now... sit quietly for a moment. Just close your eyes and let your mind be still - just for a minute. I'll wait...

Okay, what were you thinking about during that little break? I don't suppose it was a green striped apple, was it?

Chances are, it was. At least for part of the time. It's human nature to think about what we're told not to think about. Like "Don't think about that itch." And as you're telling yourself not to think about it, you are still thinking about it. So you're still focusing your energy and attention on it.

When you're thinking about what you don't want, you're not thinking about what you **do** want. And when you're not thinking about what you do want, you're not doing anything toward making it a reality.

If you're thinking about how you don't want to be sick any more, the emphasis is on being sick and you're not putting your energy toward being well. If you're thinking about how you're fed up with not having a job, you're not spending those moments or that energy doing something about finding one. If you're thinking about how you don't like the situation you're in, you're not thinking about ways to get out of it.

So think about being well, having that job you'll love, being in a situation that makes you happy. See it, feel it, imagine it, visualise it. Take all of those "I don't want this any more" thoughts and change them into thoughts of what you do want.

That's the only way you're ever gonna have a chance to get it.

77. Listen.

Listen. Stop making any noise at all for a moment and just listen.

What do you hear?

Bustling traffic and sirens? Children giggling or arguing about whose turn it is?

Office sounds, phones ringing, fingers on keyboards? Someone griping, another needing more coffee, music playing?

Listen a little more closely. Television droning, voices in a nearby room, birds outside? Ticking clock, barking dog, faint church bells?

Close your eyes and listen again. Never mind all of those external sounds. Whatever you're hearing in your environment, check it off the list as 'noticed' and listen again.

Listen to the sound of your breath. Focus on its gentleness, its evenness, in... and out... in... and out... Feel yourself relax as you sit, eyes closed, listening to that beautiful, hypnotic rhythm.

Listen to your body. Tune in and listen to what it's telling you. Does something ache? Is something sore? If so, is there a message with that pain? Is your body very tense and tight or is it comfortable and relaxed?

If you're feeling tense and wound up, focus again on your breath. Close your eyes and just for a few moments, pay attention to nothing but your breath. Imagine that you're inhaling peaceful energy that floods your whole being, and as you exhale, see all the tension and worry flowing out of you.

Keeping your eyes closed, push aside the noise, push aside the work, just for a few moments. There is only your gentle breath, filling you with peace and relieving you of the tension. Breath... after breath... after breath...

After a minute or two, listen to your body again. Listen to yourself. In this settled state, what little bits of wisdom are coming to you? Your "Higher Self" is always speaking to you, but you can only hear it when you are calm and receptive.

You don't have to have a half-hour meditation to achieve that state. You don't have to sit in the lotus position and get leg cramps while chanting "Ommmmmm".

It takes only a moment or two to ignore the external 'noise' of life and focus on going inward, if for no other reason than to enjoy the stillness it brings.

Not only will you feel a sense of peace and calm in those brief moments of stillness, doing this every now and then throughout a busy day can help to keep your stress levels down. It helps to keep you focused and relaxed as you make your way through the list of things you must get done, and it makes it easier to cope with the rush and noise of a hectic life.

And in that stillness, if you check in and ask yourself if there's anything you need to know, or ask about a particular situation that's troubling you, answers will come. Sometimes immediately, sometimes not. But you'll never hear them if you don't tune out the noise, and tune in to the stillness.

It can take 30 seconds. It can take a minute or two. Doing a handful of these mini-meditations every day can make a world of difference to your overall sense of peace and relaxation, to keeping you focused, and to allowing you to hear the answers that you can only get from the wisdom of your Higher Self.

And all you have to do is... listen.

78. The challenge of unconditional love.

There is no greater power than unconditional love. It is the purest expression of the Divine spirit that resides within each of us, a spirit that connects us to the Divine Source of Creation - and therefore, to everyone else on the planet. I like to think of us as being individual rays of the same sun.

I invite you to practice being unconditionally loving for two weeks and see how you get on. Make a commitment to send only loving thoughts and energy to anyone who crosses your mind. Do not allow yourself to have any judgemental or critical thoughts. Keep your heart and mind focused on loving the perfect Divine spirits that inhabit the human bodies of all those with whom you interact, or who cross your mind.

In all situations, remain focused on being unconditionally loving. In fact, focusing on being unconditional love. When you do this within your own interactions and situations, it becomes easier to extend that unconditionally loving energy into the wider community and then to the whole of the earth.

The concept of loving unconditionally sounds so simple. Yet in our humanness, it is often very difficult to give love in this way because we struggle to let go of our judgement and ego, the self.

It is especially difficult when we, or our loved ones, have been very badly hurt by the actions - and especially the deliberately hurtful actions - of others. How are we supposed to love those who have caused such terrible pain?

We can do it by remembering that hurtful behaviour is the result of the ego's emotional wounds and weakness. If we look past the ego, we can love the perfect Divine spirit that it hides. I'm not suggesting you should love the behaviour, just the spirit that is stuck somewhere behind it. You must separate the two.

I'm not suggesting it is necessarily easy to get to the point of unconditionally loving someone who has caused you great pain. But nor is it necessarily as difficult as you believe it to be. When you make the effort, you strengthen your own spiritual connection. And the more you strengthen that connection, the easier it becomes to love unconditionally.

And so begins a powerful and healing cycle.

When you become unconditionally loving in all your thoughts, in all situations, in all your intentions, you heal your own life as well as the lives of others.

It will also begin to remove limitations and restrictions in your life, allowing you a better view of the possibilities that are available to you, and giving you the best chance to make your dreams come true.

How about giving it a try for two weeks? Make every effort to be unconditionally loving with people and in situations you find to be challenging. That is how we grow - by stretching ourselves beyond our limits.

You may stumble, you may not always be successful. Yes, it might be hard sometimes. But so what?

The benefits will be well worth the effort.

79. Every boat needs an anchor. Every anchor needs a boat.

Just imagine being a boat. Imagine the freedom...floating across the water, drifting while the waves rock and soothe you, miles from the shore, nothing but sea and sky as far as you can see.

You can go anywhere, nothing holding you back as you're just being a boat, bobbing along all alone and wondering what your next adventure will be.

And every now and then, you just want to stop, enjoy that exact spot. You cut the engine, and rely on the anchor to hold you in place so you can rest.

Soaking up the sun and solitude, the peace and privacy, your anchor lets you love and absorb as many beautiful moments in that one happy place as you want.

If you were a boat, just think of all the wonderful places you could see. Travelling from one port to another, experiencing new sights, different cultures, faraway lands.

Such a beautiful variety of music, the delicious aromas of new and unusual foods wafting through the fresh air. The lights, the sounds, how exciting! How magical!

Your anchor allows you a longer rest, to stock up on fuel and supplies. To see to a little maintenance here and there, to be sure you're in perfect running order.

And then you're off again, carrying your anchor with you once more.

There are those of us who are boats, freedom-lovers, curious seekers of newness and change, adventure and learning, wanting expansion, to be more, find more, do more.

And there are those of us who are anchors, steady and stable, no need for newness or adventure. The anchors among us have a freedom of their own, the kind that comes from contentment with who they are and what they do. And in that contentment, there is peace.

At times, those of us who are boats need the anchors to hold us steady, to give us some stability, some perspective, to remind us to pause and reflect.

And at times, those of us who are anchors need the boats to give us a sense of purpose and strength, to remind us of imagination, creativity and possibility.

We need each other, we boats and anchors. For all our many differences, in that, we are the same.

80. From victimhood to victory.

There are many horrors inflicted by one human being upon another. Then to hear acts of violence or cruelty as "people behaving like animals" really bothers me because it insults creatures that never kill just because they can. Animals do it for survival. They don't plot and scheme and conspire and hire others to do their dirty work.

And they don't violate trust for their own selfish pleasures, robbing children of their innocence and making the world a terrifying place of abuse.

Over the years in my work as a counsellor, then a homeopath and a psychic/medium, and in my personal life, I've been shocked to learn just how many people have been sexually violated as children. What has been more shocking is that in many cases, they don't even realise it - as in my own case. As children, we think our environments are 'normal'. We're hard-wired to trust our parents; it is our survival instinct at its strongest.

I'll never forget the day the "A" word was dropped right smack in the center of my life. The day a psychologist listened to the reasons for my ending a marriage, then listened to some details about my background, and promptly - but ever so gently - asked if I knew I had been abused. Not just in that marriage, but going back to my earliest years.

I felt as though my life, everything I knew, everything I believed, everything I trusted, had been blown apart and was lying in a million little puzzle pieces on the floor. I didn't know what the picture was supposed to look like, so I couldn't imagine trying to put them back together.

And I was sure that with so much damage to my soul, many of those pieces would be missing anyway, leaving me with gaping holes that could never heal.

But I was wrong. Thank heaven I was wrong.

I thought I would feel like a victim forever. But that was before I learned why I felt that way in the first place.

Abuse, whether physical, emotional and/or sexual, makes children feel worthless. They feel dirty, disgusting, inherently flawed and "bad." In their egocentricity, they believe they deserve every rotten thing that happens to them.

In their trusting little hearts, they cannot differentiate between the abhorrent behaviour of an adult and their own value and perfection as spiritual beings.

Chances are that they will carry these beliefs into adulthood and will continue to find relationships that are unhealthy. They'll hook up with partners who demean them, are controlling, abusive or toxic in some way because in the deepest parts of their souls, they believe this is all they deserve.

It is only when they understand that they did not deserve the abuse they endured as children, and that it was not their fault, that they begin to take back their power.

When they can begin to heal the damage to their self-esteem, self-image, self-worth, and understand that the perpetrators of the abuse were at fault, they feel an emerging sense of strength and value.

Imagine that you're wearing some yummy new clothes that you love. You think you look great. You feel fab in your new threads, confident and seriously hot.

You see a complete stranger who says, "I wouldn't be caught dead wearing that. It doesn't look good on you at all."

You might become angry, indignant. Who the heck is this moron? Who asked for his opinion? And who gives a rat's @$$ what he thinks anyway?

But then your partner sees you and says, "Oh, I don't think that outfit suits you at all. I don't like it." You're crushed. You wanted him to think you look splendiferous. You might contemplate taking your new clothes back to the shop. Your confidence is shattered. You think you look like a weenie and don't want anyone else to see you looking like this.

It is human nature to want to please the people we love. And this is why we take their actions and opinions to heart. And this is how we end up feeling like we deserve to be abused. "There's something wrong with me. If only I hadn't done this or that. I must be a very disgusting person if they did this very disgusting thing to me. I deserved it; I should have known better."

That kind of thinking leaves a person feeling like a victim. "Come on, do it to me again, I deserve it." And so that person keeps finding people who will validate the belief, "I'm a victim. I am trapped, helpless, powerless."

It is only when we understand that what other people do to us is not about us. Their choices are their own. And if they've chosen to be abusive, they are the only ones responsible for it.

We enter this world as pure and perfect spirits in little human bodies. We do not deserve abuse of any kind by anyone at any time. And therefore, we are not 'victims' unless we choose to think of ourselves that way.

There are some people who prefer to live like that, people who have been told the abuse was not their fault, people who have heard that there is hope and help, that they don't have to feel like that any more.

But they prefer their 'victimhood.' It allows them to stay stuck, to get attention, to get sympathy, to be dependent, to wait to be rescued and not take responsibility for their own lives, their own healing, their own happiness.

But for those of us who want to be happy, to move forward in life and to find peace and healing, we reject holding onto the sins that have been committed against our perfect souls, because to do anything else is to perpetuate them ourselves.

We seek wellness, find our strength, stand up for ourselves and refuse to allow any further attacks on our vulnerability, which is so precious, so beautiful and so perfect.

There is hope. And I can promise you, there is healing.

You just have to want it.

81. You've already endured what you fear the most.

Have you ever noticed that what you fear the most is often something you've already experienced? I've thought about that a lot and for the most part, it's the truth. There are some things I fear which fortunately, I've not had to endure. At least, not yet.

But the person who is terrified of abandonment has already been left at some previous point. The person who is terrified of being attacked has already survived it and been left traumatised. The person who fears rejection has already felt the sting of that big, horrible NO.

Take a moment and think about some of your biggest fears. Are they, in fact, experiences you've already had? You're terrified that they'll happen again?

Well, here's the good news. If you're still standing - if you're able to read this - then you survived it. No doubt it was awful. Worse than awful. But you're still here.

And okay, you don't want to go through that nasty pain again but even if you do, you'll live.

Even if you don't necessarily feel it, you're stronger for having survived it. And heaven forbid it happens again, that strength will get you through it easier - and you'll be stronger still.

Fear can immobilise us. It can be debilitating. It prevents us from experiencing many wonderful parts of life. No one likes to experience painful or difficult situations but we do heal. But those nasty bits are part of the deal if we're gonna be here and enjoy the good stuff.

Your fear is really just a memory of the trauma. It's being locked into the feelings you had about the event that hurt so much. But having the fear -

that memory - doesn't mean the event will ever happen again.

And even if it does, you survived it once. You'll survive it again, and you'll come out the other side even stronger than before.

82. Risking failure is the only way to find success.

Throughout my life, both personally and professionally I've met countless people who have a fear of failure. Many of them had never even thought about it until the subject came up and there it was, smacking them in the face.

I'm not talking about that little bit of 'wanting to do well' or 'not wanting to fail an exam.' I'm talking about a fear of failure that creates problems. The kind that drives people to work far too hard and too much. The kind that stresses students, pressuring them to try for perfect grades, no mistakes.

It's the kind that compels people to be perfectionists, which doesn't have to show up in every area of their lives either, but it will be there somewhere. Perhaps only in schoolwork or career. Perhaps only in the way they keep their homes, their rooms, their drawers and cupboards, their collections of CDs, their rows of shoes. To make a mistake is horrible for these people. They feel terribly ashamed and stupid. They can't stand to disappoint anyone by producing a less-than-perfect result in anything they do

It's the kind of fear that makes people be competitive, driving them to be the best, to beat the other guy at everything they attempt to do. Terribly demanding of themselves, they expect to get the best marks in the class, the best job performance evaluation, the best praise from parents, partners, friends, volunteer organisations - they need to be "the best", the winners, the ones who accomplished the most. To be less than the best is unacceptable; the pressure must be unbearable after a while.

It's the kind that makes people fear failure to such an extent that they dare not even attempt to succeed. They feel as though there is no way that they could cope with getting it wrong, with not reaching the goal, not being successful - whatever that means specifically. Afraid they'll make a mistake or they won't be the best or get it 100% right, they don't even bother to try.

If they aren't absolutely certain that they can do it exactly right and be perfect, they won't do it at all.

And so, we end up with wasted brilliance, wasted lives, wasted opportunities, wasted creativity. There might have been miracles in the making. But we will never know.

What is it that could make people feel this way? What could possibly be behind such a debilitating fear?

It is another fear, an even bigger one. It is the fear of not being loved, or the fear of being rejected, being abandoned - all of which are tied up in one another. Somewhere deep inside, there will be an issue like this, a deeply-rooted fear which then leads to the fear of failure and its resultant behaviours.

"If I could just be perfect, or be the best, then I would be good enough - then I would be loved and I would not be rejected or abandoned."

The problem is, you can never be perfect. There is no such thing so you set yourself up for failure right away. And although you may be the best at some things sometimes, you will never be the best at everything all the time. And therefore, you set yourself up for failure this way, too.

So what can you do about this? Examine why you feel that fear of failure. What is it that needs healing? Are there rejection and abandonment issues that you can identify? They don't have to be physical abandonment issues either.

For example, it may have been that a parent was emotionally unavailable to you, even if you were in the same house.

There could be a million reasons for it so I cannot speculate about all of them here. The point is to look at the fear of failure. Dig deep and see where it begins.

Then find ways to heal the wounds that are causing it, through affirmations, self-help books, surrounding yourself with loving people, through journal-writing, spiritual guidance, meditation or any other way that will help you.

You can give up the fight to be perfect or to be the best. You can turf your fear of failure because you're already just as good, just as perfect as everyone else on the planet. On a human level, all of us mess up, all of us make mistakes. Granted, some of us make a lot more than others, but so what? As I've said on numerous occasions before this one, behind human behaviour, its foibles and flaws, there is always a perfect spirit. It resides within us and it guides and directs us - when we let it.

When we get caught up in human foolishness like greed, jealousy, envy, dishonesty, or something really silly like believing we're undeserving of love, that's when we run into trouble. We must remember that we will always have all the love we could ever want, as long as we accept ourselves and love ourselves first.

If you don't think you're lovable, you will never feel the love that is given to you. You will reject is because if you think you are not lovable, you would not believe that anyone really loves you; therefore you will not feel it, no matter how many times someone says "I love you" and no matter how much love you are shown.

You will be like a bottomless pit of need and emptiness, aching for someone to fix it, for someone to love you - when they do - but you don't believe you deserve it...and so you don't feel it... I'm sure you can see the chicken-and-egg problem with this.

We are all deserving of love. We are always loved by someone, and usually by many 'someones'. Depending on your spiritual beliefs, there is Universal love from a Divine Source available to all of us, flowing through us and around us all the time.

We can choose to feel that love which is pure and unconditional, and let it heal those human wounds of rejection, abandonment and unworthiness. We can let it heal that human need to be perfect, to be the best, and accept ourselves as being perfectly imperfect, as humans should be.

When you can reach that point, you can love yourself unconditionally, which will allow you to move forward in your life, taking risks, trying and failing, trying and succeeding - but a whole new world will open up to you once you understand that you are still lovable and still as perfect as a human can be, remembering that mistakes are inevitable. There is no shame in making them. And besides, they are opportunities to learn and should be welcomed.

If you won't risk failing, then you don't try at all. That's called 'giving up' - and isn't that failing?

Risking failure is the only way you will ever find success.

83. Self-sabotage...is it your 'thing'?

Yesterday, I wrote about the fear of failure. Today, I want to tell you a bit about a related fear - the fear of success.

It sounds impossible. Why would anyone fear success? Isn't that what everyone wants? Isn't that what the fear of failure is about? Not being successful?

Aren't people working themselves to death trying to earn more, be more, accomplish more, to make their parents proud, their spouses proud?

These two fears have the same roots. So many of us have had childhood issues or other life experiences which have left us feeling inadequate, undeserving of anything good. I'm always running into people who say things like "I'm stupid" or "I'm such an idiot."

When I point out what they've said, quite often they'll say they didn't realise they'd even said it - what a shame... But it's very true that many of us are really good at negative self-talk - and it's incredibly destructive.

To make such comments in the first place, there must be an underlying belief that they are the truth. To say them over and over again only reinforces that belief.

We carry with us the memories of our failures, our disappointments, the disapproval of others, especially of those who are or were in positions of authority, or whose opinion has been very important to us. And when we "failed" those people, it hits us at a very deep level.

So why, then, do we fear success, when failure feels so bad?

It's precisely because of those damaging beliefs about being a disappointment, being a failure, believing that we'll never amount to anything, we don't deserve anything good, we're stupid.

We will always surround ourselves with people and situations that will validate what we believe about ourselves. So if we don't believe we deserve or can achieve success (whatever that might mean specifically to each of us), we continue to make choices that will ensure that we don't get it.

And this is where self-sabotage comes in. Sometimes we're aware that we're doing it, but more often than not, we have no conscious awareness of the fact that we're making sure we don't become successful.

When things are finally going well, when we're on the right path with a career, or when it looks like that relationship is finally going to be the one we've always wanted, we do something to mess it up. And we do it because we don't know how to be successful. We can't imagine ourselves like that. We have no vision of it, can't feel it, wouldn't know what to do with it.

What's worse is that we're really good at a lot of things. All of us have our strengths. But then there's that one failure. That one area of weakness, the one place where it went wrong, and perhaps in a big way. And that's what we focus on.

It's like if we hear 25 great things about us, and then one negative remark, guess what we remember??

So there you are, focusing on the places where you went wrong, and forgetting the places you went right. Or perhaps you haven't even gone wrong yet but you've heard throughout your life that you can't do anything right, or for whatever reason, you just don't believe you could do anything well, and you believe you can't get there.

Perhaps not succeeding is your thing. You're in your comfort zone with that. It's familiar to mess things up; this is your identity and it's all you know.

So you shoot yourself in the foot - every time it looks like you might actually prove yourself (and possibly others) wrong, because it starts to feel a bit scary when it looks like it's all going well. You start to wonder when it's going to go wrong. You don't trust that it will continue to go well. You start waiting for the other shoe to drop.

And when the other shoe doesn't drop, when things keep going well, you become increasingly nervous about it. You can't trust it. Things always go wrong, so this will too, right? And the nervousness builds and it's all very uncomfortable because there is no drama, there's nothing going wrong, it's all going right but this just can't be, this doesn't happen to you, because you always get it wrong.

It gets so uncomfortable that you can't stand it any more. You quit waiting for the other shoe to drop and instead, you pick it up and slam it hard on the ground. There. Done. Thank heaven you don't have to wait for that any more.

Then you tell yourself - and everyone else - "See? I knew that wouldn't last, couldn't last. It always goes wrong for me, see? I was right."

If this sounds like you, start looking at why you believe you shouldn't, can't or won't be a success. Start examining where those beliefs came from.

Chances are they're rubbish opinions from parents or teachers or bullies on the playground or some jerk boss or boyfriend - or some combination of these and heaven knows what other influences from your life experience.

Whatever their origin, those beliefs can be changed.

You're always free to change any beliefs that don't work for you.

Once you've identified the ones that keep you from success, then look at what it is you do to validate them. Look at your patterns. What is your self-sabotaging behaviour?

Then start imagining being successful. See yourself in the life you want. Just get a picture of it in your mind. Imagine how it would feel. You might want to create a vision board, using a collection of pictures from magazines or off the internet to represent the life you want.

Keep it where you can see it regularly; it will help to reinforce the vision that you've got in your mind. It will help to keep you focused on where you want to be.

Change your language. Change your thoughts. Every time you hear any negative self-talk in your head, change it. Replace it with positive thoughts of deserving, strength, success, empowerment.

If you keep doing what you're doing, you'll keep getting what you've got. If you're tired of what you've got and you want something better, and you can see that you're sabotaging your own efforts to get there, you have the ability to stop - and take that first step toward reaching your goals.

No, of course it won't happen overnight. These issues can have very deep roots. But with those, you just have to dig a little deeper and yank a little harder, and they do come out with some effort.

You have to start somewhere, right? So start by examining why you keep choosing to self-destruct. Then put one foot in front of the other...and you will begin to walk down a new and much happier path that leads to success.

84. A suicide takes more than one life...

I stayed in bed late this morning, not at all interested in getting up after a restless night. Nestled in my soft featherbed, listening to the quiet morning sounds of this sleepy little village, my world was snug and warm, and very safe. The rooster across the lane kept urging me to get up. The cows told him to be quiet. The birds sang me back to sleep a time or two.

But eventually, the rooster won. I left the peace and comfort of my delicious bed and within minutes, was reminded of how quickly things change in this life. I received the shocking news that my little sister had found her husband after his suicide.

He'd made another attempt just last week but followed it with words of apology, saying he didn't mean to do it and would never do anything like it again. He was in hospital for a day or two but they believed him and sent him home. He convinced everyone that he wouldn't do it again.

Eventually, he convinced them that it was safe to leave him alone for just a short time.

This time, he chose a sure-fire method. This time, he wasn't going to get it wrong. He would see to it that it was as permanent as the gruesome memory that his young widow will now carry with her forever.

He's left her confused, and his children, too, with his family feeling guilty, feeling responsible, filled with regrets and 'if onlys'. They will have to work long and hard to accept that it was not through any fault of their own, that they are not, in fact, responsible. That they had no control over his actions and are not to blame. Such is the legacy of a suicide...

They will struggle with their anger - and their guilt about their anger, both of which are perfectly normal but it's easy for someone on the outside to say that. It's another matter entirely to believe it when you're directly affected by it.

They will struggle to understand what he was thinking, and how he could have ended up in such a dark and terrible place. They will struggle to imagine how he could have done what he did, and not to imagine him preparing and actually doing it. They will struggle not to be tormented by wondering if he suffered and what his last moments were like.

I know that side of it; I have lost special people to suicide, too. But I know, too, how it feels to be that depressed. I've reached that point more than once in my life.

The last time was the worst. It was many years ago but I will always remember it very well. I had been unbearably ill with a life-threatening condition for such a long time, I couldn't take it any more. I couldn't bear the physical suffering and I felt like a huge burden on everyone around me. So I made a plan.

Typical of people who attempt or commit suicide, once I had that plan, I felt better. I was happier than I'd been in ages. I felt peaceful, knowing I had a way out of the suffering. I just needed to find the right time.

But my patients still needed me. As long as I could help them, I was still of some use in the world. And so, somehow I carried on, putting one foot in front of the other every minute, and the minutes became hours and the hours became days. After a few weeks, I managed to pull myself out of that terrible hole. I can't tell you how relieved I am about that now...

So I understand both sides of it. I've been the one left behind, and I've been the one wanting to go. And on both counts, I know I'm not alone.

Sometimes we meet people who are constantly threatening to kill themselves. Sometimes it goes on and on and happens over every little drama and eventually, we don't believe them any more. We say they just want attention. We say it's "just a cry for help." Then they make a half-hearted attempt and sometimes it is minimised - again, "just a cry for help."

But it's not "just" a cry for help. Okay, perhaps they don't really want to die, but maybe they don't want to live any more (there is a big difference). Or maybe they just hurt so much that they don't know how else to say it. Maybe they don't know where to go for help, or maybe they just need to know someone cares because they feel so desperately alone and unlovable.

We mustn't get frustrated with people who behave like this; instead, we must try to find out what's wrong and see if there's a way to get the help that they need. But of course, these people have to be willing to help themselves. Sometimes they are, sometimes they are not - they just want to be rescued.

But all talk of suicide must be taken seriously - just in case an attempt is made. Sometimes attempts are only meant to be half-hearted and death wasn't really on the menu but it happens anyway.

About 25% of the time, there is no warning. There are those people who just up and do it without talking about it. The suicide occurs out of the blue, and sometimes there isn't even a note. They were here one minute, and gone the next.

But there are many cases where there are plenty of signs. It is important to know them and hopefully, you will be able to spot the potential for suicide in someone who is on the edge and contemplating or planning it. These are some of the signs:

* Appearing depressed or sad most of the time

* Talking or writing about death or suicide

* Feelings of helplessness or hopelessness

* Rage, shame, guilt

* Drug or alcohol abuse

* Withdrawing socially or from family

* Feeling trapped in a situation

* Impulsivity

* Changes in mood or personality

* No interest in anything, especially favourite activities

* Changes in eating or sleeping habits

* Giving away favourite belongings

* Talking about Wills, insurance policies etc.

If you know someone who is struggling with this issue, take it seriously. Be as supportive as you can be and see if you can assist in finding the appropriate kind of help for the specific issues that have led to these feelings.

If you are depressed and having any thoughts about ending your life, remember that it is a permanent solution to temporary problems. Although you may be feeling like you'd be doing everyone a favour by checking out, that is your depression talking. There is always hope. There is always help. There is always support - you just have to look for it, or accept it when it's offered.

Life is so precious. Sometimes it's bloody hard, too. But the hard parts always pass. The only constant is change. I would never have believed I could be well again, given how ill I was all those years ago when I had decided to check out. The odds were very much stacked against me and recovery seemed hopeless.

But I had a miracle. And if I'd given in to my desire to end my life, I would have left behind a large group of devastated family and friends. I would have missed so many wonderful experiences with them. I would have missed the best part of my life - the part where I found my way to happiness.

Whether you're the person contemplating it, or dealing with someone who is, don't give up. Don't give up. Don't give up. There is no second chance when they try till they get it right...

85. Have a Daily Planning Meeting with your intention.

One of the best gifts you can give yourself is a short period of silence every day. Amidst the talking, the telly, the chattering, the busy-ness, the phone calls, the traffic, the noise in your head just ***stop***.

Think of it as the 'Morning Planning Meeting' with the boss - although it doesn't have to be in the morning, if you have to hit the ground running. You can wait till it all settles down in the evening - or any other time when you can give yourself just a little bit of uninterrupted time every day. But the point is still the same.

So who's the boss? It's you. Your Higher Self. Your inner wisdom. Your intention. "The boss" can get lost in the shuffle with all the noise and busy-ness of your life. You can get bogged down in concerns of the ego - what you need right here, right now, what you have to get done, who said this or thinks that - and you get caught up in your human existence and daily 'stuff'.

Meanwhile, "the boss" is yelling outside your office door, but you're engaged in an argument with someone or watching some mindless television or you're busybusybusy with your job or the shopping or the children.

You might be aware of that voice trying to push its way through the noise but it doesn't really register until finally - blissfully - you can give yourself a few moments of silence. A little peace. A short period to shut out the world and let the boss have a word with you.

That "Planning Meeting" is essential if you don't want your days to run amok. Just a brief little check-in to remember or re-set your intention about the kind of person you want to be, the quality of life you choose to have, a reminder to pursue peace, to offer help, to be loving and patient as you

215

make your way through each day.

It doesn't take much and it doesn't take long. It doesn't even require any effort or any money. Quite simply, it requires you to be still and quiet, for just a few minutes (or as many as you wish).

Just give "the boss" a chance to help you prioritise, organise, and to remind you of what your job is, and to keep you focused on getting it done.

That little Planning Meeting will make your job a whooooole lot easier.

86. What anyone else thinks is none of your business.

Chances are, you enjoy having your own thoughts, your own opinions. Chances are, you don't appreciate anyone telling you what you should think about anything. Chances are you don't like it when someone tells you what they believe you think - especially when they're wrong.

Well, in the heads of all the other people on the planet, it's the same. They'll enjoy having their own thoughts and opinions. They'll not appreciate you telling them what they should think about anything. They'll not like it when you tell them what you believe they think and you insist you're right - and they'll especially not like that when you're wrong.

They don't have to agree with you and it doesn't matter who's right - and there might not be a 'right' or 'wrong' anyway. You can cram your opinions down their throats all you want, and it doesn't change the fact that they're entitled to have all their thoughts to themselves - just as you are.

If you expect others to feel like that about you, then you must give them the same respect in return and quit bothering yourself with what anyone else thinks. If it's people who really care about you, they'll support you even if they disagree with your choices. If not, why would you care what they think?? You'll be tearing your hair out for nothing.

So cut yourself a major break and just let it go. They're probably too busy with their own lives to really think much about what you do anyway.

The bottom line is quite simple. What anyone else thinks is none of your business, just as what you think is none of theirs.

87. A little message with a big meaning.

I am still breathing today. And if you're reading this, so are you. Whatever else is going on in your life right now, as awful as parts of it might be, you're still drawing breath.

And that means there is always hope. And you can live a long time on just a little bit of that.

As bad as it is today, picture how it could be better. Picture what you want for yourself. That is the first step toward making it happen. The next step is to find even one small way to put yourself a little bit closer to making it your reality.

When you keep doing that, a little piece at a time, eventually you'll get there.

88. Self-love and self-destruct are incompatible

As all of us know, life can be very difficult. Worse for some than for others, but all of us have our own struggles.

How we get through them depends upon a variety of factors, such as life experience, spiritual or other beliefs, and how strong our support systems are.

One of the most important aspects of coping with stress and life's challenges is how you feel within yourself, and about yourself. Do you feel a sense of turmoil? Are unresolved emotional issues eating at you? Do you feel like a failure? Is there a steamer trunk filled with self-esteem issues strapped to your back?

If there is some element of these kinds of problems overshadowing your life, it is easy to be self-destructive, especially when faced with the challenges that lie in your path.

When you don't feel confident and at peace with yourself, self-doubt creeps in, quickly followed by negative self-talk which rapidly turns into self-criticism and guilt.

It's a short trip to self-destruct in that frame of mind. You can end up feeling like there's no use in trying, you don't deserve to be happy - or worse, you deserve the difficulties you're having - you can slide into choices that validate what you believe, and the turmoil and unrest continue. The unhealthy habits continue. The poor lifestyle choices continue.

It is only when we truly love ourselves - for all we are, and for all we aren't - that it is impossible to do anything self-destructive.

Take a look at your life - and your lifestyle. Are you consciously making unhealthy choices for yourself? Are you deliberately putting yourself in situations that are harmful to you physically, mentally, emotionally or spiritually?

Most of us do this to one degree or another. We don't exercise, we drink too much alcohol, we smoke or eat too much junk food. We stay in unhealthy relationships, allowing partners to belittle us or control us, we don't get enough sleep or enough playtime.

Can you see any self-destructive tendencies in your own behaviour? If so, perhaps a little chat with yourself is in order to try and determine its origin. Perhaps you already know. Perhaps you need a little help in figuring it out.

Once you're aware of the cause of your self-destructive actions (or inactions), focus on self-love. Begin treating yourself as though you deserve to be loved, respected and valued, even if you don't believe it 100% to start. It might feel a little strange at first, but stick with it. Treat yourself as if you're someone you adore, someone you idolise.

Find ways to address the deeper issues. There are a ton of self-help books available; there are support groups, chat rooms, blogs, all kinds of ways to find help and healing. Whatever it is that is at the core of self-destructive behaviour, I can assure you, you are definitely not alone. Healing is possible - if you want it.

The goal is self-love and inner peace, and once you reach it, you will be unable to harm yourself or anyone else. Now isn't that a goal worth reaching?

89. "My dog ate my homework."

"I'd love to help out but I have to go to this Thing…"

"I wish I could but I've got a prior commitment."

"I've been meaning to do that but I've just been so busy."

And the least imaginative (i.e. the laziest excuse) of all, "I can't. I have to wash my hair."

The list goes on and on. We can all be really good at making excuses when it suits us. But what exactly does that mean? Why would it "suit us" to make excuses?

That's easy. We're afraid of something.

"Oh, no," you might be thinking. "Not every excuse is about fear!"

Oh, yes. It is. Every single one of them will be about a fear of something.

There are the excuses we make when someone asks us to go to some event or other and we have absolutely no interest. But we're afraid we'll offend them, or they might not like us, or they'll be angry or insulted. We don't dare just say "No, thanks."

There are the excuses we make when we're dating but discover behaviours or attitudes that we just don't like in the people we've been seeing, and we decide we don't want to see them any more. They suggest getting together and we avoid their phone calls, or tell them repeatedly, "I can't, I'm busy that night" until they finally figure it out and quit asking.

Or we might go so far as to tell them as gently as possible that "…it's just not working out." But when they ask what we mean, we say "It's not you…it's me" when we know perfectly well that's not at all how we really feel. But we are afraid to be honest, afraid to hurt their feelings, afraid to stand up for ourselves.

Then there are the Mothers of all Excuses. The ones we tell ourselves about why we can't do something that benefits us. Why we can't pursue our goals. Why we don't take chances, let opportunities slide past us, walk away from our dreams.

We tell ourselves we've just been too busy lately or it would cost too much or it would upset someone if we got this or achieved that. We're loaded with excuses that we sugar coat as "reasons" so we can cram them down our own throats, foolishly thinking that others can't see the truth about our cowardice.

The worst of it is that most of what we fear won't happen anyway. And it's usually just based on self-destructive and inaccurate beliefs such as "I'm a failure; I'll fail at this, too." Or "Nothing good could happen to me. I know it won't work out so I'll save myself the disappointment."

Excuses are always dishonest. They're a feeble attempt to hide – or at least ignore – the truth. And the truth is always about fear.

When we make decisions based on fear, there will never be a good outcome. It restricts growth and learning. We stay stuck in the same place, thinking the same thoughts, having the same experiences, fearing the same things as we've always done. We cannot move ahead if we don't take risks, be honest, face the truth about who we are, how we feel, what we want and need for our lives.

And that is a terrible waste.

The next time you hear yourself about to offer an excuse to anyone for anything – including and especially if it's to yourself – stop and think about what it is that's keeping you from speaking the truth. Try to determine why you're doing your level best to shoot yourself in the foot. Examine the fear that has twisted itself into an attempted justification for the excuse you are about to make.

It is only when you face that fear and address it that you will be able to continue on the journey toward being all you're meant to be.

90. It doesn't matter who believes in you, as long as you do.

Have you ever had an idea about something you wanted to do, then told someone who said, "Hmmm... I don't know about that" while wearing a doubtful expression? Have you been on the receiving end of someone giving you a list of reasons why it wouldn't work, shouldn't work, might not work?

Have you ever told someone excitedly about an achievement, something you were thrilled to have accomplished, only to have that person shoot it down with the ways in which it could have been better?

Could you feel your shoulders droop, your face fall, your heart sink as those negative words dragged your spirit into a dark and murky place?

Many years ago, I was married to a man who told me about an incident when he was just a young lad at school. He was so excited to have got 98% on a difficult exam. He went burning home after school, couldn't wait to show his mother, who looked at him and said "Where's the other 2%?"

It broke my heart for him because I had been living "up close and personal" with the damage that such comments had inflicted on his soul. I wanted so desperately to heal those wounds, to help him erase that pain. I'd had similar experiences so I could relate to how he must have felt, and what this had done to him for years afterward.

All of us have been disappointed by the words of others in our lives. All of us know what it's like to want others to believe in us, to encourage us, to support us. We want others to be excited for us when we're setting out on an adventure, trying something new, being brave and pursuing our dreams.

Yet we forget that those people have the same kinds of wounds that we have and sometimes, those wounds make them say things that we don't expect and don't much like. Those people are unable to see our accomplishments or our potential because they can't see their own. All they can see are their own failures and pessimism, because that's what's been pointed out to them, or it's been their life experience - or both.

We put a lot of emphasis on needing and wanting the support and encouragement of our friends and family. We want them to believe in us. But we forget one very important point. We don't believe in ourselves.

It's bad enough when someone else wants to rain on your parade, but when you do it to yourself, that's a big problem. As much as we want the approval, acceptance or support of other people, we have no control over what they'll say to us about anything we do. We can never be sure when their own demons won't pop up and smack us in the face. And because we're already struggling to believe in ourselves, we believe those demons instead.

If you go to others to improve your self-belief, you're asking for trouble. You can't believe in yourself because of what anyone else says or does. It's always your own choice. Even if absolutely everyone around you is blowing off an idea you've got, you've still got the ability to believe in it, to believe in yourself. No one can take that away from you - unless you hand it over on a silver platter.

The bottom line is this: How can you expect anyone else to believe in you if you don't believe in yourself?

91. "I'm leaving without you then, and I'm never coming back!"

I used to see it fairly often, back in the days when I had occasion to be out and around in shops a lot, raising a bunch of children and having lots of errands to run. I saw it, too, when women friends would come round with their little ones. And I still see it, although less frequently as I don't have a lot of reason to be in situations where it occurs.

I'm talking about those moments when you're in a shop and a child is busy looking at something, probably a little toy, and Mummy is ready to leave.

"C'mon, Jonathan. It's time to go."

Jonathan keeps playing with the toy.

"Jonathan, let's go."

He continues to ignore his mummy.

"Jonathan, I'm in a hurry." The tone is stern now. "Come on, put that toy back and let's go!"

Jonathan might whine at her or maybe he continues to ignore her but he does not put the toy back and does not make a move toward leaving.

Impatiently, Mummy says, "Fine, then, I'm leaving without you," and turns toward the door.

Little Jonathan is petrified! Dropping the toy, he runs to his mummy screaming, **"No!! Mummy!! Don't leave me!!!!!!"**

Clinging to her leg, he sobs all the way to the car...

This is, unfortunately, a common event amongst mummies and children. I've seen children not want to leave my home, and then their mummies threaten to leave them with me forever, and then make a move toward the door. It's everywhere. And it's a dreadful thing to say to a child.

There's a reason why the offspring of many species bond with their parents. They need that bond for their survival.

And so it is with people. Children need to bond with parents to feel safe, to be able to develop emotionally, to be well physically.

There is something called "failure to thrive." It happens to babies and very young children when there is a nurturing issue and they don't eat and/or don't gain weight, become sickly, and sometimes even die.

When that bond is threatened or broken, it creates a deep sense of abandonment in children. They become insecure; the world is no longer a safe place and suddenly, anxieties and fears spring up out of nowhere.

On a very deep level, they fear what will happen to them if their parents leave them. Where will they live? What will they eat? What bad things will happen to them? Who will take care of them?

It is terrifying.

It's bad enough that we read frightening stories to our children - stories like Hansel and Gretel, about a greedy stepmother insisting that the father should take his children deep into the woods at night so they're lost and can never come home.

The story goes from bad to worse when they end up with a wicked old witch who wants to eat Hansel - but fortunately, they escape just in the nick of time.

There's Snow White, whose jealous stepmother sends a hunter out to remove the girl's heart. When that fails, she poisons the young woman.

There's Rapunzel locked away in a castle; there's the promise of giving up a firstborn in Rumpelstiltskin. Story after story, we tell our children stories of abandonment by parents in one way or another.

And we wonder why they have nightmares. We wonder why they develop into anxious, nervous teens or young adults - we wonder why we, ourselves, have felt insecure on some level, for as long as we can remember.

Those bedtime stories only feed what many children are hearing out of the mouths of their own parents. "I will leave you." "Go away." "I'm sick of looking at you, get lost." "I wish you'd never been born." "You were an accident."

Whether or not these things are said in jest, or in an impatient moment of frustration, children take such comments to heart. Threaten a child's safety and place in the family, and you set that little person up for a life of insecurity and feelings of abandonment.

This can (and often does) cause all kinds of unhealthy and self-destructive behaviours, especially in relationships.

Control issues, needing to please, being fearful to speak one's own mind, promiscuity, jealousy, eating disorders, substance abuse, selfishness, feelings of inadequacy and low self-esteem, becoming very needy or clingy, being dependent - the list goes on and on.

Even if everything else in a child's life is loving and predictable and safe, with just one threat to "leave you here forever!" you can do some serious damage to a fragile little soul that depends on you for its very survival.

Be careful what you say to children. They take things very literally and they're extremely trusting. They do not always understand a joke.

Nor do they know you don't really mean that you'll "leave them there forever", especially when you're saying it like you mean it, in an effort to get them to do what you want.

You want them to believe you. And they do.

92. Can you put aside your own squeamishness in order to support someone in need?

There are times when family or friends call upon us to do something for them and it is something we don't think we can face. I'm not talking about being asked to break the law or to willfully hurt someone, or anything like that.

I'm talking about situations in which people need us to do something difficult, something that frightens us or that overwhelms us, like sitting with them in a hospital during a horrible test or treatment. Being there during a traumatic Court appearance for a sexual assault. Or perhaps identifying the body of a loved one.

It can be especially difficult if what they're asking is something that pushes our own buttons, triggering memories of some trauma from our own lives, or putting our own fears right smack in front of us.

What do you do in situations such as these?

Unfortunately, many people cannot - or will not - put aside their own fears, their own memories, or their own discomfort and agree to help. They have a choice about whether or not they endure the difficult situation but the people asking for help do not. What's worse is that we may not even be personally involved in whatever that situation is. We feel for our friends, but we are not directly connected to the event.

If it's bad enough for us that we don't want to be involved, imagine how it is to be the people who *have* to be involved, who have no choice but to experience whatever it is that we find to be so distasteful. It's quite possible that you have been on that side of such a situation, needing the support of people who didn't feel as though they could stomach getting through it with you. And if that's the case, chances are that you're more willing to put yourself out for others in need, no matter how squeamish you are about doing what they ask.

Life is hard a lot of the time. And sometimes it feels impossibly, horribly unfair, too much to bear. But those times can be made a lot easier when others are willing to help us through the worst parts. Isn't that what we should be doing? If we're all in this very messy experience together, shouldn't we try to make it easier for each other?

Distasteful, shocking, uncomfortable, painful or not, certain situations will arise. When we're the ones in need, we're happy to have someone say "Yes, I'll help, I'll be there, never mind about me, this isn't about me, this is for you, this is what you need, so yes, please, let me help."

The way I see it, it is an honour to be asked to support others through their darkest and most frightening experiences, to be allowed into their lives in such an emotionally intimate way, to be trusted and respected enough that your presence makes a very powerful and positive difference in their lives. It is not a chore or a duty; it is a privilege. It speaks volumes about how you are perceived, about your importance to those people, what you mean to them.

In this way, it brings more meaning to your own life. And what a beautiful bonus - those people will never forget what you did for them. They will go through the rest of their lives, knowing that they were truly loved, that someone really cared, that they were able to find comfort and support when they were most in need.

These are among the most priceless gifts we can give - if we're willing to put our own "stuff" aside in order to help others with theirs.

93. The more you hide your light, the more we want to see it!

Do you hide your light under the proverbial bushel? Are you afraid to be seen? Do you want to be invisible?

Not wanting to be seen by others is usually not about others at all. It is usually about wanting to hide from ourselves. There is some sort of emotional pain that makes us withdraw, doesn't allow us any confidence or self-esteem. We don't want to see ourselves as we are, because we don't like ourselves. And we can't imagine that anyone likes us either.

So we try to hide ourselves from others. People say we are introverted, shy, loners. As we try to be inconspicuous, we become more noticeable because the silence and unwillingness to open up is so obvious. When we're too quiet, people don't know what to make of us. They wonder if we have a problem with them. They wonder if we don't like them. It's disconcerting to them; they don't know what we're thinking and it can keep them off balance. It creates a distance and a separateness that is certainly not helpful in forming relationships.

That, of course, is the point; there is some version of "if they knew me, they wouldn't like me" going on.

The truth is, the more we try to hide from others, the more we are seen. We attract the very thing we fear - being pushed to come out of hiding. All of us are flawed and imperfect and all of us have got a unique beauty that is meant to be shared. Our human imperfections are no worse than anyone else's and it is only when we see ourselves as equal to everyone else that we can begin to feel comfortable in letting our lights shine for the world to see.

We allow others to be imperfect; why do we not allow it in ourselves, too? We must treat ourselves the way we treat others. If we enjoy everyone else's light, we must allow them to enjoy our own.

Come out from hiding. Smile at your imperfections and if they are aspects of yourself that you can change or want to change, then change them. If not, accept them as just a part of you, but don't deprive the rest of us of seeing your beautiful spirit.

94. Looking for that "Perfect Relationship"?

Most of the songs that are recorded are about love and romantic relationships. They're about how wonderful it is because we've finally found "that special someone" or because we've either got – or lost – the greatest love the world has ever known. We spend loads of time, energy and money on finding a "perfect partner".

For many of us, relationship problems create no end of grief and pain. They distract us, make us depressed, anxious, interfere with our jobs, and can send us to the most horribly painful places we've ever known, especially when the relationship has ended but it wasn't of our own choosing.

Then we spend ages aching and hurting over it and in time, we're looking for yet another "perfect love". But there's a difficult truth about relationships that many people do not know, or refuse to believe.

The reality of relationships is that they are only ever as healthy as we are, emotionally speaking. Our relationships act as mirrors, showing us exactly what it is that we need to heal in ourselves. But we don't see this. All we know is that we're up to our necks in unmet needs, hurt feelings and crushing disappointment.

The word "health" has the word "heal" in it – and in the case of relationships, you can use "healed" or "unhealed" instead of "healthy" or "unhealthy" because a healthy relationship involves both partners being healed (or at least well on their way to healing) of the emotional wounds that have been inflicted on them throughout their lives.

Generally, we think we're pretty much okay to live with. Sure, we have our faults and our old booboos that may haunt us, but look at any personal ad or online dating profile and you'll see what people think of themselves. You get the usual assortment of stuff like "great sense of humour, fun-loving, sensitive, caring, romantic" blah blah blah.

But they don't tell you "traumatised by years of abuse, no idea how to stand up for myself, no sense of boundaries, and I let my family control my every thought and choice." They don't say, "I'm controlling, selfish, rigid, disrespectful when angry, and foul-tempered when I don't get my own way. Oh, and all of that will be your fault."

People who are living such lives as these cannot possibly attract emotionally healthy, stable, healed partners. Firstly, people who are well along the path of healing are not going to be interested in dealing with such a lot of unhealthy behaviours and attitudes. And secondly, people in such an unhealthy place aren't going to have a clue how to deal with someone who has solid boundaries and a strong sense of self-love and respect. It is impossible for such a relationship to work.

So how do we get to that happy place of healthy relationship?

It begins with *the* single most important relationship you have – your relationship with yourself. It begins with examining your own unhealthy patterns, your flaws and weaknesses, your own emotional wounds, and learning how they've impacted your relationships with partners.

Self-awareness and understanding are the keys to healing the damage from years gone by. The goal is self-love and self-respect. Then – and only then – will you have a chance to have a healthy romantic relationship because you won't be playing out all of your unresolved issues, acting on unmet needs and expecting others to make you feel whole, happy or complete.

One of the biggest problems in relationships is that we don't understand the difference between relationship issues and individual issues, and more often than not, the problems are really individual issues (our "emotional baggage", which comes from our life experience). They will be reflected in the relationship, but they are not about the relationship.

An unexamined life (i.e. those individual issues that we bring to our relationships) will continue to wreak havoc, its various wounds throwing a spanner into every relationship, sabotaging attempts to find a healthy, loving partner. It can be a terrifying thing to delve into the murky depths of our psyches and see what nastiness is crawling around in the dark and erupting under the cloak of a relationship gone wrong – when it has no possible chance to go right.

Those "mirrors" never lie. Our relationships will always reflect back to us exactly where we need healing. The first step is to uncover what the issues are. The second step is to do something about resolving them.

If you are not currently in a relationship and think you could use a boost along your path of healing, I can highly recommend Dr Phil McGraw's book, "Self Matters". It's like one-stop shopping for anyone who wants to take a serious look at those murky depths and get rid of the monsters, once and for all.

If you are in a relationship that is struggling, the good Dr Phil has also written "Relationship Rescue" which is brilliant beyond words. With loads of "cut to the chase" information and great exercises to do, even if your partner doesn't want to do the book with you, it can still be of tremendous benefit because it makes you look at *yourself*. It forces you to contemplate your own life experience, behaviours, attitudes – and your partner's as well, which can make a big difference to your own happiness, whether you stay in the relationship or not.

And whether or not you choose to use either of these books, or find help from other sources, the bottom line is the same. Unless and until you examine your own life and analyse who you are and what makes you tick, and then heal the broken bits, your relationships will only be as healthy (or unhealthy) as you are.

95. Now, where did I leave my bandwagon? Oh, here it is.

This morning I will be attending Keith's funeral. He was a lovely man, a beautiful, gentle soul, by all accounts, happy-go-lucky, easy-going and good-natured.

Deeply sensitive, he was a brilliant artist, an animal lover, and extremely sentimental. And now he has become a suicide statistic.

He was not prone to depression until recent months when work troubles, health issues and family problems began to take their toll. He wasn't in terrible shape but just didn't seem to be coping as well as he would have liked. His doctor wrote a prescription for anti-depressants and handed it to Keith without a word about possible side effects.

Within weeks, Keith told his young wife that he didn't feel right, he "felt numb, didn't feel anything at all" and wanted to go off the meds. His doctor advised weaning him off the drugs but by then, suicidal ideation had begun.

This was a first for this man. Never in his life had a suicidal thought entered his mind. Never had he uttered a word about wishing himself to be dead. Not until he took Citralopram.

After one failed attempt with pills, he spent just a couple of days in hospital and was released with little follow-up. Eleven days later, he sat in his doctor's office for a five-minute check-up, during which she later reported that he was "chirpy" and seemed fine.

But just hours later, his wife found him dead in their home.

For several years, this drug (Citralopram, Celexa or Cipramil) has been widely reported to cause suicide.

In fact, it has become such a prevalent problem in children and teens that it is no longer given to anyone under the age of 18. Prozac is another anti-depressant known to cause suicides and as far back as 2004, there were studies that indicated in children and teens, it carried a 50% higher risk of suicidal thoughts and attempts than those who took placebos. Mirtazapine is another anti-depressant that can cause suicide, especially in anyone under the age of 24.

This is not an exhaustive list. But I'm sure you get my point.

There have been lawsuits by shocked and grieving family members who have attempted to make someone accountable, yet governments are still allowing doctors to prescribe these deadly medications - and no one is insisting that patients be told of this possible side effect.

At the time of Keith's failed attempt, the hospital and the doctor should have known about suicide being a side effect of this drug, and that one attempt could very well mean that there would be another - and one which he would be sure to get right. They should have known that his cheerful smile just eleven days after an attempt on his own life was a big, red flag, as suicidal people become quite happy when they've worked out a plan and they know relief is imminent.

It's bad enough that this lovely man was released from hospital so soon, that there was virtually no follow-up, that he was told he couldn't see a counsellor for three months, that every medical professional he saw, from the writing of the prescription to the moment of his death, chose to ignore the potential for this terrible tragedy.

And of course, it is horrific to think about him having taken his own life. But it is too much to bear, thinking that if he hadn't taken this bloody drug, he would, in all likelihood, still be alive.

How many more deaths will it take before pharmaceutical companies stop producing drugs that kill people? Before governments stop allowing these prescriptions? Before doctors and other health care professionals realise that just because the risk may be small, it is still too great if there is any potential at all?

When will people start finding other ways to resolve their depression, or treat their anxiety? What about self-help? What about psychologists who help people deal with emotional issues that cause depression and anxiety? What about alternative treatments like reiki, acupuncture, homeopathy and many others? When will we stop popping pills in a futile attempt to fix problems caused by our culture? When will we take our well-being into our own hands, instead of listening to doctors and automatically swallowing their advice, never questioning, never seeking alternatives, just blindly accepting their authority and thinking they know bloody everything? Because I can assure you, they don't!

Money, power and ego run the conventional medical communities and its affiliates such as pharmaceutical companies. I don't think those are very good reasons to listen to their advice - not without asking a million questions, not without thorough investigation about options, not without making absolutely certain that it really is the best course of action.

As a culture, we have given up our power to medical professionals and their authority. For more reasons than just this tragic suicide - and so many others - I think it is well past time we took it back.

96. Mud pies and other simple joys.

Do you remember mud pies? Do you remember how delicious it was to squish that cool, soft mud between your fingers (or your bare little toes)?

There's a reason why there are zillions of nerve endings in fingertips. Think about how lovely it is to stroke the skin of loved ones, or to run your hands through their hair. We are tactile by nature, some of us more so than others. And touching things that feel nice in our hands just makes us feel good.

The idea of squishing a lot of mud through your fingers and under your nails may not appeal to you now, but what about getting your hands into some cookie dough? Wouldn't it be lovely to work all those yummy ingredients together, perhaps with chocolate chips or raisins or maybe cinnamon and cloves, which would delight your nose, too?

Then taking little blobs of dough and rolling it between your hands to make a nice little cookie? Ooo, that would be fun! And tasty, too, after they're baked. Although there are those people in the world who eat cookie dough. Ew.

For the more advanced baker, you could get your hands into a load of bread dough, working it to mix everything together, then kneading for several minutes until it is a lovely, smooth, elastic dough that you can shape into cinnamon buns, knotted rolls or simple loaves - whatever your imagination dictates.

Maybe you just want to dive into your kids' playdough. And if you haven't got kids or you haven't got playdough, there are countless recipes for the stuff on the internet. Easy peasy to make, and loads of fun to enjoy, pummelling it, squashing it, rolling and shaping it, and if you don't like how it turns out, bash it up and start over.

238

When the playdough dries, you can paint your creations. Or chuck 'em in the bin. Whatever you want, but at least you'll have had a little mental health break and it'll have done you a lot of good.

There's something very therapeutic about this mindless activity of working with squeezing and mixing stuff in your hands. It's calming, soothing and relieves stress. That's why you can buy those pretty little Oriental stress-relieving balls, some of which make a lovely chiming sound as you roll them around in your hands.

So what'll it be? Are you gonna make some cookies? Some cinnamon buns? Some playdough? Or are you gonna "get down and dirty" and go and find some mud to squoosh around for a while? If you're worried about looking like a weenie, find a kid and presto, there's your excuse to play.

97. It's not what it takes to knock you down; it's that you get back up. AGAIN.

There's no doubt about it. Life gets in the way of our desires and our dreams, sometimes on a very regular basis. And sometimes in some pretty nasty ways. I'm sure there are few people on the planet - if any - who have not known heartbreak, crushing disappointment and dashed hopes.

There are some of us who have been knocked back so many times, kicked in the head, slammed onto the pavement by the stuff that gets thrown at us, we've lost count. Some of us might feel like our lives have been nothing but one long struggle. I've been one of those; I know how it feels.

After a while, you might start to feel like there's no point in getting up again because you just know something, somewhere, is going to shove you back down. And then it gets a little worse when you reach the point of thinking you can't get back up again. You're exhausted. Fed up with the struggles. Fed up with swimming upstream for your whole life and never getting anywhere.

But if you don't get back up, what is there for you? If you keep yourself there on the pavement, flat out and fed up, giving up, not bothering, done trying, what kind of life is that?

You might ask, "Well, what's the point of getting back up again, making the effort, trying again, when I know I'll just end up back here?"

The point is, at least that way you have a chance of things improving. Think of it like a slot machine. You put in your coin and pull the handle. Nope, didn't win. Another coin, another pull. Nope. Another coin, pull again. Nope.

And you're thinking, "Just one more. Just one more. Odds are that this time, it'll work. Once more."

And you can't stand to walk away, knowing that with every pull of that arm, it is increasingly possible that the next one will be the winner. And if you walk away now, there's a good chance that someone will sit down in your seat for that next pull and the machine will start spitting out tons of money - including all of your coins.

So you try again. Just this once. One more time. Maybe this will be the one...And eventually, there is the payoff. Eventually, the machine does cave and give out tons of money.

Well, life is like that, too. You try and you try and you try, try, try, and get no result, or just a little result or an almost result and you keep trying and being defeated or derailed.

But the only way you're ever gonna hit that payoff and be rewarded for your patient and persistent attempts is to put in another coin and pull that handle yet another time.

While you're busy feeling deflated and derailed, see if you can spot patterns in your attitudes or behaviour that are contributing to your efforts being thwarted repeatedly. Are you hanging out with people who are negative?

Are you filling your own head with negative self-talk and self-destructive thoughts and language? If you keep believing it will all go wrong, you'll continue to set yourself up to make it happen and validate your beliefs - without even being aware of it.

Some of what flattens you will be related to external circumstances over which you have no control - the death of a partner, your employer going bankrupt and you're out of a job, an Act of God that washes away your home in a flood.

But there are plenty of difficult circumstances that are in your control. How you choose to live your life, whether or not you choose to examine your attitudes, your reactions, your behaviour, whether or not you want to understand where they come from and how they affect your life, and whether or not they need to change - and whether or not you follow through with that change.

These are the kinds of things that need to be tackled so that when you do pick yourself up again, you set yourself off on a better path than you were on previously. You improve your chances that one day, Life will stop slamming you into the pavement, or will at least tone it down to a tolerable level.

The only way you can ever have a chance for that to happen is if you get back up again and keep fighting for the life and the happiness you want. Lying flat out on the pavement will only get you squashed.

So get up - again. One more time. You can do it. Yes, I know it's exhausting. Yes, I know you're sick of it. Yes, I know you feel like everything you ever try will fail. Yes, I know you don't want to try any more. Yes, I know you think there's no point.

But there is. You still have a pulse. You're still breathing. That means you still have the opportunity to make improvements in your life, to change the things that you can, to accept the things over which you have no control, and to stop defining yourself and your life by everything that goes wrong.

Envision what you want for yourself and your life. See it, feel it, hold that vision in your heart and in your mind. Never let it go. And get back up again, whether you want to do it or not. You deserve to give yourself another chance.

98. A fresh start is good for the soul.

I have a love/hate relationship with mornings. It takes me ages to wake up and get moving, now that I don't have to hit the ground running with a bunch of children any more. I'm not good at daytime. I detest being out in the sun; I prefer grey, misty days. I love the dark and am very much a 'creature of the night'. Mwa ha ha ha haaa.

I love the early morning hours when the sun has just come up, the air is crisp and cool, there's dew on everything and the world smells fresh and clean.

I love those hours the most if I've been up all night, which I would do regularly if it didn't mess me up so much because the rest of the world doesn't live like that.

But as much as I drag my sorry behind first thing in the morning, and as much as I don't like sun or daytime after about 8 a.m., there is something to be said for those very early hours, 5, 6, 7 a.m.

With every sunrise, it is a new day. The early morning dew has given everything a rinse and renewed hope; it's a fresh start, a chance to begin again. If you've never thought about it like that, just go and sit outside for a little while during those sparkling early hours in the morning sun, and see

for yourself. On such a pretty day, it is impossible not to feel the refreshing and rejuvenating energy of the universe as it shows you its promise.

It is the promise of another chance, of wiping the slate clean, of leaving the past where it belongs. It is the promise of finding your way forward, of becoming who you're meant to be, of creating the life you want for yourself.

It takes your agreement and participation to fulfill that promise, but the universe offers it every single morning, with every single sunrise, with every new day. It offers you a chance to put yesterday out of your head and ponder possibilities for today, tomorrow and the rest of your life.

Every beautiful new morning gives you a chance to put things into perspective, to let go of the small stuff, to heal what needs healing, find courage where you need encouragement, to put the past away and lock the door on it.

A fresh start. A chance to begin again. What a wonderful gift and how lucky we are to get one every single morning.

99. The most difficult journey is inward.

I find it interesting that many people are afraid of any meaningful self-analysis. They don't want to become any more self-aware than they already are, which is often on a fairly superficial level. They don't really know what makes them tick, nor do they care. They're content to just carry on doing whatever it is they do, whether or not they're happy, whether or not their thoughts and behaviour get them into trouble. They live on "leave well enough alone."

I reckon that's okay if it really is "well enough" but quite often, it is not. Quite often, they're wandering through life, dragging their emotional wounds with them, like steamer trunks full of pain, insecurity, fear and feelings of inadequacy.

On the surface, they think they're happy. Or at least they don't notice if they're not.

They don't notice how that steamer trunk is planted right smack in the middle of the road ahead of them, affecting various aspects of their lives. And it's also planted right smack in the middle of the road inward, the one that leads to self-awareness and understanding. The one that leads to healing.

They stare at that steamer trunk with trepidation, fearful of what's inside, as though they'll lift the lid and some horrible, creepy monsters will leap out at them and tear off their heads. "Better left locked up," they decide. They'll just park there, at the side of the road, and be content not to go any further. "Self-awareness? No, thanks. Too scary."

Beyond the steamer trunk is a big, dark closet. They peer past the trunk but can't see anything and that's okay because they don't really want to know what's hidden in that closet. They're sure it can't be anything good.

And in part, they're right. In part, there will be some bits that aren't nice. All of us have them. But there's also a whole lot of great stuff. There's wisdom in there, there are insights you didn't know you had.

So you bite the bullet; decide to risk it. At least a little. You're not ready to turn on the big, bright bulb that's hanging in that closet. Maybe just shine a flashlight in there as you journey inward. The further you go, the more you discover about who you really are, how you feel about things, honestly and bravely facing the truths about your Self.

Yes, it can be a bit unpleasant in there and you won't always find things you like. But being aware of them can make a monumental difference to how you live your life, how you treat others, how you treat yourself, and whether or not you move forward and progress to places of happiness and fulfilment.

And you can be sure you'll also find lots of wonderful goodies in there, too, places of beauty and strength, wisdom and insight and you will be amazed by how much you didn't know you knew. You'll discover just how far you've really come, just how radiant your spirit really is and you will be more willing and able to let the rest of us see it, too.

The journey inward is one of the most frightening journeys we can ever take, but it is also one of the most rewarding. Personally, I don't fear it. I embrace it. I love it. Muck and all, I'm happy to keep discovering more and more about myself so that I can fix the yucky bits (or stop letting them interfere with my life, at least), and I can make good use of the best bits.

I don't really understand why we should ever be so afraid of ourselves as to not want to know ourselves intimately. What makes even less sense to me is that in that state, so many people complain that their partners don't understand them. Well, how could anyone else understand them when they don't understand themselves?

Most of us wish we had partners who will love and accept us unconditionally, flaws and all. But how can we expect anyone else to do that when we don't dare look at our imperfections ourselves? If we think we're so awful on a deep level that we don't even want to know, how on earth do we dare expect anyone else to accept us as we are?

To me, that's about as hypocritical as one can get. "I don't love myself, I don't fully accept myself because there's no way I wanna dig around in the murky depths of my psyche, it's scary in there, but my goodness, I'm gonna find Mr/Miss Right to love me perfectly and no matter what, and he/she will always be there for me and will think I'm wonderful and will accept all my quirks and flaws, even if I'm too scared to find out what they are. I don't wanna know but they have to love all the yucky stuff I don't dare look at."

Does the word "Duh..." spring to mind?!

It's not that bad, taking that journey, when you balance the yucky bits with the good stuff. It's just you in there, so how can it be that bad? Believe me, it's gonna be a lot of the same kind of stuff that everyone else has. We're not that different from one another. We share a lot of fears and flaws and we can all be really awful and really wonderful.

Come on, be brave. Be willing to shove aside that steamer trunk and turn on that big, bright light in the closet. You're the only one who has to know what you find, unless you choose to share it. So what's to be afraid of?

100. Could I have some help please?

It is one of the most difficult questions in the world. It's not as hard to ask when we're doing it on behalf of someone else. But when it's for ourselves, it is a whole other ball of wax.

For some of us, it is an issue of vulnerability. "I am showing weakness if I cannot do everything for myself, if I need anyone for anything. If I show weakness, my enemies can hurt me."

For others, it is an issue of deserving. "I do not matter, I don't deserve to have other people go out of their way for something I need."

Still others fear rejection. "If I ask and they say no, I'll feel like they don't care and don't like me."

There are lots of reasons why people don't ask for help. Yet many of them don't mind being asked by others. In fact, some people thrive on it.

One of the hardest lessons I've had is the one about asking for help. I grew up in an environment where my needs didn't matter, my feelings were inconsequential, and I was ridiculed or criticised for having "bothered" anyone with them. I was pretty much left to fend for myself in many ways.

This was especially true when I was asking - and in fact, begging - to be protected from regular attacks by a family member. But my requests were ignored and the violence continued. So I stopped asking.

I felt as though I was very much alone in the world. I believed I wasn't worthy of receiving help. I believed I was just a bother and had no right to ask anyone else to go to any trouble to assist me. And even if someone offered to help, I had a terrible time accepting it.

I grew up and became someone who was always available to others in need.

"No matter what, day or night, just ask and I'll do it" - that was how I lived. Like a big ol' beacon to a million moths, I attracted all kinds of people who took advantage of my willingness to help others. My phone rang in the middle of the night, people dropped by at all hours, and as much as I was able, I gave and did and listened and helped and gave some more.

It took a lot of years before I learned some valuable lessons about that. One of the most important was the difference between people who genuinely need help, and those who just want to take whatever they can get. But that's another topic for another day...

What I want to address here today are the issues that prevent people from asking for help, and if you are one of those people, ask yourself why. Chances are, your answer will be related to some longstanding emotional wound, although you might not identify it as such.

But take a closer look. What do you believe about asking for help or accepting it when it's offered? Where did those beliefs come from? Do you hold the same beliefs for others? Or do you have a different set of "rules" for others who need help?

We are all in the same boat. We're not really so different from one another; all of us hurt, all of us grieve, all of us want to be loved and accepted. All of us experience pain and loss, frustration and fear, anger and anguish. All of us need help at some points along the way, even those of us who act like we're tough as nails, or who seem to be as independent as anyone can be.

It may be quite possible to get through life without asking for help - or accepting it when it's offered, but I should imagine it's a lot more difficult that way. And a lot lonelier. We are social creatures; that's how we were built. When we help each other, we create and strengthen emotional bonds. We feel like we have support systems that will help us weather the many storms of life.

I thought I would need great healing before I would be able to ask for help. But I realised that it was in asking for help that I would be healed. I had to do the thing I feared in order to prove to myself that I was worthy of receiving help, that people saw me as valuable, that I would not be personally rejected because I needed something. I had to risk hearing "no" to discover that usually I would be given a resounding "yes".

I started with the "safest" people, the ones closest to me, the ones I trusted and who I knew genuinely loved and cared about me. The more I asked, the more I saw that there had been nothing to fear in the first place. People were quite happy to assist me. And when there was the occasional "no" in response to my request for help, I didn't take it personally any more.

Next time you find yourself needing help but choking on the request, ask yourself why it is so difficult. See if you can identify what gets in your way. Then challenge yourself to push past that obstacle, go to someone you trust, and make the request come out of your mouth. I promise, it does get easier with practice. After all, we need each other. If you're always there for others, isn't it time you allowed them to be there for you, too?

101. Gratitude.

I've always admired and respected people in particularly nasty jobs. Like nursing, for example. I imagine it's a rather thankless job, for the most part. Dealing with sick people, who can be grouchy and miserable because they feel awful and they take it out on anyone who comes within ten feet of them... I remember writing 'thank you' letters to the nurses in hospital after I had my babies because I always had complications and a couple of times nearly died. I was so grateful for the patient and loving help I received from the nurses when I was critically ill.

Later, I found out that almost no one does that. Almost no one writes to thank them for the care they provide.

But they show up day after day, putting on their best smiles, being as loving and giving and compassionate as they can, and they must go home at night utterly drained, and wondering if anyone they helped even noticed that there was a person inside the nurse's uniform.

When I still had children at home, I used to have a gratitude journal on my kitchen table. All of us wrote in it every day (and so did anyone else who came by, if they felt like it), even if it was only one line and even if it was something silly, a small thing like "I'm grateful that I had ice cream today."

I met someone once who thought this was a terrible idea. "Disgusting", in fact. I asked why but he was in such a knot, he wouldn't even answer. He didn't even let me tell him why I did it.

The reason I wanted to teach my children about gratitude was to help prepare them for life. I knew full well that it is sometimes excruciatingly painful and dark, that it can be terrifying, lonely and desperate. I knew that when it gets like that, all you can see sometimes is the awfulness.

But having some perspective and being able to see the good in your life can help to get you out of that terrible dark hole.

That old saying, "count your blessings," is so important. Not in a way that is admonishing like, "You should consider yourself lucky, young lady!!" But in a way that allows us to find balance when we're drowning in misery. In gratitude there is hope, because we see that life is still worth living, that all is not lost, and this can give us a boost and help us to feel better.

Letting people know that we appreciate them or what they do is important because we all like to know we've made someone's journey a little easier, that our time here is not wasted. We like to know we've made a difference. Not for our own sakes, but for the people we have helped.

Their gratitude adds meaning and purpose to our time on this planet. With or without it, we can carry on, doing what we do, helping where we can, making someone smile, making a rough time easier, being the helping hand that we've sometimes needed ourselves, supporting and sharing with each other and trying to make the best of what life throws in our paths.

But it is nice to know that we have touched the lives of others, or that we have made a difference, and that our time on this planet has been well spent.

And so, I am thanking you, all of my readers, from the bottom of my heart for taking the time to read my blog and my books. I'm thanking those of you who recommend them to anyone you think might benefit from my words. I appreciate knowing that my difficult life and my learning have been put to good use in helping to make the journey easier for others.

I thank you, too, for all the heartwarming emails and messages that you send, the comments you leave on Facebook, telling me you're finding some help, some hope, some food for thought, and sometimes a little stroll down memory lane or perhaps a chuckle or two by reading what I've written.

It means the world to me to know that my very difficult life is now being used to make other people's journeys a little easier. I'm glad to know there was some purpose in it beyond my surviving it.

Please know that I'm grateful to each and every one of you for spending some of your precious time with me by reading my words. I thank you from the bottom of my heart.

ABOUT THE AUTHOR

To say that liberty is quirky is something of an understatement. She loves bare feet, the moon, red peppers, old stuff that's falling apart, and misty days. She adores creaky things, giggling, crunching crisp dead leaves, and covering her ceilings with years' worth of her children's precious artwork. She worships silliness and does her very best not to be too much of a grown-up unless absolutely necessary. One of her children has often said it's very hard to parent her.

Enduring an abused childhood led to an extremely turbulent life with far-reaching consequences. She has struggled with abusive and dysfunctional relationships, life-threatening health problems, and has overcome a lengthy battle with anorexia, as well as an addiction. She has lived the hell of parenting nightmares that you see in films. And so much more.

Eventually leaving Canada and moving to England, liberty became a British citizen, intending to spend the rest of her life in a quirky, 500-year-old cottage in rural Northamptonshire. But after several years, Life happened and the universe wanted her back in Calgary to begin a new life.

As a single mum in the 1980s, liberty returned to school and studied social work, later becoming a hypnotist to further help her counselling clients. She has used her experience in these areas to produce a number of guided meditation CDs for healing, to stop smoking, lose weight, find pain relief and so on. In the '90s, she studied with the well-respected School of

Homeopathy (Devon, England), eventually earning her Practitioner's Diploma.

Her greatest passion is writing on a variety of topics, often with a spiritual thread. She was blessed to secure a top literary agent in London who is currently seeking a publisher for some of her work.

She is also an artist and has enjoyed several exhibitions of her mostly abstract and expressive work, which has been sold internationally

She has worked as a professional psychic and medium, doing readings in person, and over the phone or in email for people in many countries around the world. Taking to the stage in England, she connected audience members with loved ones in spirit.

For five years, approximately monthly liberty was a guest on Sue Marchant's evening show for BBC Radio Cambridgeshire, which is broadcast to nine counties in the east of England. During these appearances, in her capacity as a psychic and medium liberty took questions from listeners.

She has transformed a life of pain and suffering into one of strength and healing, doing what she can to help people take control of their lives, let go of the past, move forward, pursue their dreams and feel fulfilled.

CONTACT THE AUTHOR

libertyforrest.com

facebook.com/libertyspage

twitter.com/libertyforrest

smashwords.com/profile/view/libertyforrest

OTHER BOOKS BY THE AUTHOR

At the time of this writing, liberty has published, and will be publishing several other books in both print form and as ebooks, some of which are listed below.

"The Power and Simplicity of Self-Healing" - after extensive research, this book offers indisputable proof that all of us are capable of healing ourselves of virtually any ailment.

We've all heard those occasional stories of people who have recovered from untreatable or incurable conditions. There are those who were told they would never walk again - but through sheer determination, they did it. There are those who were riddled with malignant tumours and given a death sentence, but repeatedly visualised perfect healing and they became well.

There are numerous documented reports like these and usually, we think they are flukes, coincidence, or perhaps "miracles". They are so rare and so powerful, the notion that this could be commonplace does not occur to us.

But it should.

The "default setting" for any living organism is survival, yet it is only possible if the organism is inherently able to heal. We think nothing of our ability to recover from illnesses, injuries, broken bones. But why stop there? Why is it impossible to believe that we can heal ourselves of anything more serious than a broken arm or a really bad flu?

It is only because we have not known we could do it. For thousands of years, we have turned to medicine men, healers of all kinds throughout the ages, unaware that each of us possesses the power to create - and to heal - our illnesses.

"The Power and Simplicity of Self-Healing" is chock full of fascinating information that revolutionises the way we look at illness and healing. This life-changing book encompasses a wide range of seemingly disconnected and unrelated subjects, yet each one is a separate piece of an incredible and complex puzzle. One at a time, liberty explains each of them, ultimately revealing a startlingly simple picture that provides indisputable scientific proof that all of us have the ability to heal ourselves of virtually any illness.

For most of her life, liberty suffered with ill health, some of it life-threatening, much of it just plain miserable and debilitating. For a number of years, she had found great help with homeopathy, believing it to be the be-all and end-all in healing. Although it is extremely powerful and produces miraculous cures, she reached a point where it was no longer helping, nor was anything else. She had run out of hope and any reasonable options. Her desperate and futile search for wellness had taken her down many paths from the conventional to the near insane.

When it seemed all avenues had been exhausted, in an explosive moment of anger and frustration, she vowed to find a way to heal herself, believing that if other people have done it, then she could do it, too.

With occasional interjections about her own story of suffering and healing, this book covers a multitude of topics in a step-by-step systematic fashion, layering one piece of information on another and building a strong foundation so that all of the pieces are well-connected and logical.

Drawing on a wealth of information from numerous medical professionals, researchers and scientists, along with the metaphysical, mysterious and inexplicable, liberty drops one fascinating piece of the puzzle after another into its rightful place, creating multi-faceted and undeniable proof that self-healing is not only possible and powerful, but very simple for anyone to do. If she can do it - as ill as she was - you can do it, too.

"Incredibly interesting and informative! So fantastic, I didn't want it to end. A truly life-changing book."

-- Katie McAlindon, Kettering, England

"Wow! What an amazing book!! Definitely a must-read. It's completely life-changing, helped me to alter my whole way of thinking. I feel like a newer, happier and more positive person. Just what I needed. Perfect!"

-- Ashleigh Marshall, Northampton, England

"Incredible as it seems, using substantial scientific evidence, this book proves that we do have the POWER to heal ourselves, IF we have the knowledge. This book provides us with that knowledge in everyday, down-to-earth, layman's language. Everyone should read this book."

-- A.M. Kandiuk, Toronto, Canada

"The Spirit Within": A collection of short stories

You know, as unique as each of us is, all of us are very similar to one another as well. How often have you felt as though no one could understand what you are experiencing? Have you ever wondered what

possible reasons there could be for our journeys and our struggles, or how spirituality fits into them?

Have you ever wondered 'How will I cope with it all'? Have you ever tried to make sense of the pain that Life seems to continue to throw your way? Do you ever feel like Life is just a series of difficult lessons?

For all of our differences, we are also very similar, yet sometimes, we feel very much alone and misunderstood

Inside this book, you will find a collection of short stories, some of which are purely about our human struggles; others look at them from a spiritual perspective, offering possible answers to many of your questions. The title story, the last and longest in the book, is especially thought-provoking and inspiring, offering meaningful and powerful insights that make sense of the difficulties we encounter in life.

There are very short pieces about grief, and being lost in the depths of depression, along with more uplifting pieces, such as a delightful story simply entitled "Hope." Time and time again, you will relate to the feelings, the struggles, the triumphs and life lessons that you will find in this book. It looks deceptively simple on the surface, but there is a depth and richness to the stories that has surprised many in its former life as a print book and published under a different name.

Take a little walk down the common path of our human existence, and find yourself elevated to the spiritual plane, where you just might experience comfort, hope and healing in ways that you've never experienced them before.

"Outstanding! There are really no words to adequately describe what liberty has written in this collection of short stories. Only someone who has come back from a higher plane could know as much as she does, especially as seen in the title story, 'The Spirit Within', which is the last in the book. liberty uses a very unique style of story-telling to convey many experiences to which all of us can relate.

"I believe liberty forrest is one of the literary geniuses of our time. I have never read anything as wonderful in my life. The stories in this book are stylistically different, and spellbinding.

"This is no ordinary woman; she has been to the spirit world before, and has revisited us to learn more lessons in life and to teach us what she has learned. She is a truly remarkable woman and writer.

"An entertainingly, brilliant read."

-- Pat Bradley, Cheshire, England

"The Gift" is a heartbreaking, emotionally charged novel. It is the story of a family's journey through a very difficult and turbulent year. Already having endured many hardships, this family is fractured without even realising it until the youngest child becomes critically ill.

With Christmas approaching, the little girl's health takes a dramatic turn for the worse. Her parents and brothers quietly begin falling apart and it doesn't take long before the fractures are enormous cracks, threatening to shatter the family completely.

Four-year-old Angelina watches as her family is forced to confront its demons, and she longs for her parents and brother to find their way to healing. But as with many healing journeys, things must get a lot worse before even beginning to get better.

This story is certain to move its readers to tears as they connect and identify with each member of the Lane family. Meet Angelina and the others: Wife and mother, Kathy, so lost in her own emotions that she withdraws from life, entirely in denial; her husband, Robert, guilt-ridden and feeling inadequate; teen son, James, consumed by his own anger to the point of self-destruction; and Elijah, a wise old soul at the age of ten, trying desperately to be the glue that holds his family together. Follow these troubled hearts, who are lost and struggling to find their way through the darkness and who have lost all hope of ever finding the light.

"This is a wonderful, endearing book, with all the ingredients to stir your imagination and lift your hearts. The story tells a tale of how each member of a family deals with a difficult emotional situation. It will wring your heart out like a sponge, and yet it is beautifully orchestrated, showing raw emotions and how the family members deal with their own demons. I was so deeply moved by this book, I have ordered a copy for every member of the family and all of my friends!

"With an exceptionally emotionally charged ending, I cannot say enough about this book. It leaves you wanting more, wishing it didn't end, wishing you could know more about what happens to this family. (The author) is so descriptive and lets us known the characters so intimately, that we cannot help but feel that they are real people and we really want to follow their lives after the story ends...

"If you never buy another book again, you must buy this one! It is so powerful, so moving, so beautifully written, it is guaranteed to be an extremely satisfying read!"

-- Mrs. Charles Senior, Bolton, England

"A very inspirational book. The characters pull you right into the story and keep you reading. I laughed, cried, and was in awe. Truly a wonderful writer!"

-- Melinda L. Clarkson, Oregon, USA

INDEX

40.   On living an empowered life

41.   Challenge yourself. You're worth it.

42.   Books, covers, judgements and treasure boxes.

43.   If you keep doing what you're doing, you'll keep getting what you've got.

44.   Oh, dear! What will the neighbours think?

45.   Don't reduce your dreams to fit your reality. Expand your reality to fit your dreams.

46.   There's nothing quite like a delicious little cuddle.

47.   Good day! Or is it? That's entirely up to you!

48.   Do not diminish your pain, your accomplishments or your life because of anyone else's.

49.   On fearing change

50.   If you say it, mean it. And if you mean it, prove it.

51.   Little kids know some pretty cool stuff.

52.   Where are Ted and a blankie when you need them? Right under your nose.

53.   You can't help someone who doesn't want it.

54.   Don't push the river. Be the river.

55.   Think yourself into wellness.

56.   We believe we create intention. But intention creates us.

57.   Oops. I crashed and burned. Again.

58.   Arguing is a good thing. Until...

59.   Damn. Mother's Day. Again.

60.   Finding your voice in the midst of change

61.   Laughter is the best medicine.

62. Go for it now. Tomorrow is not a sure thing.

63. Playtime Report.

64. Be open to how you can serve. Be a Miracle Worker.

65. People are presents.

66. To be able to ask for help is a blessing.

67. Another way to let your light shine.

68. You are a duvet that cannot be put back in the bag.

69. For the love of nourishment

70. If you're struggling to get to "happy", you can at least intend "relief."

71. A bit of Karma for the mini-Hitlers in our midst.

72. Two wrongs don't make a right.

73. There's your side, their side, and the truth.

74. You can't heal till you know what needs healing.

75. If the mountain won't come to Mohammed...

76. Don't think about the green striped apple.

77. Listen.

78. The challenge of unconditional love.

79. Every boat needs an anchor. Every anchor needs a boat.

80. From victimhood to victory

81. You've probably already endured what you fear most.

82. Risking failure is the only way to find success.

83. Self-sabotage...is it your thing?

84. A suicide takes more than one life...

85. Have a Daily Planning Meeting with your intention.

86.   What anyone else thinks is none of your business.

87.   A little message with a big meaning.

88.   Self-love and self-destruct are incompatible.

89.   "My dog ate my homework."

90.   It doesn't matter who believes in you, as long as you do.

91.   "I'm leaving without you then, and I'm never coming back!"

92.   Can you put aside your own squeamishness in order to support someone?

93.   The more you hide your light, the more we want to see it!

94.   Looking for the "Perfect Relationship"?

95.   Now where did I leave my bandwagon? Oh, here it is!

96.   Mud pies and other simple joys.

97.   It's not what it takes to knock you down; it's that you get back up. Again.

98.   A fresh start is good for the soul.

99.   The most difficult journey is inward.

100. Could I have some help, please?

101. Gratitude

Made in the USA
Charleston, SC
02 November 2014